The Gift

Katherine Valentine

DP Publishing
Woodbury, Connecticut

DP Publishing

The Gift
Copyright © 2012 Katherine Valentine

For further information:
DP Publishing
P.O. Box 608
Woodbury, CT 06798

ISBN 978-0-615-59814-7

PRINTED IN THE UNITED STATES OF AMERICA

April, 2012

First Edition

Cover photography © Montalbano Photography
Edited by Eileen Denver
Design by Bonnie B. Stephens

The Gift

Katherine Valentine

Also by Katherine Valentine

A Miracle for St. Cecilia's

A Gathering of Angels

Grace Will Lead Me Home

On a Wing and a Prayer

County Fair

The Haunted Rectory

Dedicated to my dear friend, Shirley Derito

An angel of light

The Gift

Chapter 1

The Ministry of the Holy Rosary Is ...

– *A vessel of hope and healing to all who suffer*

ॐ

Many years ago, my husband Paul and I were invited by friends to attend a healing service in a small non-Catholic church. It was an informal affair. A minister spoke briefly about the power of faith to heal, and then two prayer teams gathered at the front of the church to lay hands on those wishing prayer.

Paul and I were seated toward the rear of the church, and so we had an unobstructed view of those who had lined up for prayer. Some of their ailments were openly visible—a man using a walker, his face tight with pain; a woman wearing a scarf encasing a bald skull. But the needs of most gathered for prayer were visible only by the look of deep fear and sorrow etched on their faces. As they made their silent trek toward the altar, I counted off prayers along my Rosary, each prayer wrapped in a petition that those seeking healing would find comfort and a renewed faith in God's grace.

I was the only one with a Rosary in hand in this Protestant church, yet location has never concerned me when it comes to using the Rosary. Throughout some of life's greatest storms, the Rosary has been my anchor, holding me steadfast in faith regardless of the depth of the heartache or the sorrow that surrounds me.

I long ago discovered that, as I travel along the beads, the Mysteries become a bright, shining beacon of hope that highlights God's great, eternal love and that helps embolden my faith during times of great crisis.

Through the Joyful Mysteries, Mary shows us how even the lowliest person's simple 'yes' to God's call can help save a world. The Sorrowful Mysteries remind us of the lengths that God will go to restore us to Him. The Glorious Mysteries speak of the awesome power of our Father to overcome any obstacle, even death, reminding us that nothing we experience can ever be outside His power to save. In the Luminous Mysteries, we reaffirm the Divinity of Christ as He established His Church and our 'oneness' with our Savior through the Eucharist.

I pondered these thoughts that day.

The church had grown quiet except for those praying up front. I joined my prayers with theirs, reflecting on the power inherent in our combined petitions, asking our Holy Mother, through the power of her intercession, to draw close to those among us that day who suffered.

As I fingered the beads, I happened to notice a homeless woman enter the opposite pew. She was dressed in several layers of ill-fitting coats so it was impossible to make out her shape, but she appeared to be quite large. Beneath a woolen cap, the woman had tried to capture a mane of silver curls without much success. Strands of tangled locks stuck out in mad array.

Carefully, she laid her rather large stash of full plastic bags in the pew, then gave a cursory glance around the sanctuary with the practiced gaze of the street-wise, as if sizing up the people gathered in the space. Finally assessing that her belongings would remain safe, she made her way toward the rear of the healing line, shuffling forward in shoes that were several sizes too large.

I have a special love for the poor and downtrodden, so I stepped up the prayers, asking the Lord to meet what appeared to be a myriad collection of needs. Patiently, she waited as one after another petitioner came forward within a circle of outstretched arms to have hands laid on their bowed head and prayers said on their behalf.

Finally, it was her turn. I smiled, envisioning the comfort that she would take from a warm out-flowing of Christian love. I'd once read that one of the most painful issues the homeless encounter is the absence of human touch.

The leader of the group noticed her advance and stepped forward. Bending slightly, he whispered something in her ear, and then pointed toward the back pews. Even from a distance, the message was clearly discernible. There would be no prayers said for her.

My first reaction was one of anger. How could they turn this poor, dispirited woman away? And they called themselves Christians?

Then I realized that I had no way of knowing the history between the woman and this group. These healing services were held monthly. Had she come before and caused a disturbance? Did she have a history of violence or erratic behavior that would have taken away from the solemnity of the service? I simply didn't know.

But this I did know. I had never felt such despair for another human being as I did for that woman that day.

I watched, heartsick, as she turned to retrace her steps. She didn't protest, probably because this was not the first time that she had been shunned. Tucking her chin into her chest, she bowed her head in resignation and silently walked back to her seat. All eyes followed her slow progress. Finally, this broken woman slipped into the pew across from me, leaned forward and covered her face with her hands.

I stepped up my prayers again, asking our Holy Mother to deliver the poor, wretched woman from whatever ailment had led her here. Then Mary spoke to my heart.

Give her your Rosary.

The silver Rosary clutched in my hands had special significance. I had wanted a silver strand for decades. Years before, a woman at Mass had a beautiful silver Rosary that I admired, but that I knew was much too expensive to ever dream of owning.

Then, on my birthday, my husband Paul surprised me with one of my own. It had been imported from Italy, with thick beads and a crucifix that lay across a lattice background. I am seldom attached to 'things,' but I dearly loved this Rosary and never removed the strand from its case without sending up a note of heartfelt thanks.

My first thought as I looked at the poor homeless woman was that Mary must mean one of the plastic Rosaries in the back of my car that I had bought for CCD. But, as soon as the thought surfaced, I felt Mary's words move across my soul. This time, however, they came with a new insistence and were very specific.

Give her your silver Rosary.

Much to my shame, I began to rationalize and list all the reasons this would not be a good idea. The woman wouldn't appreciate the value of such an expensive Rosary. Certainly, a plastic one would do. After all, this was a Protestant service. The woman probably wasn't even Catholic and would have no understanding of its significance.

Handing over my most cherished Rosary was a major sticking point, but I was even more reluctant to make such a public display of my faith. Sharing my faith in such a public place wasn't something that I felt comfortable doing. What if the woman refused the offer? I'd never done anything like this before.

And what about the other people gathered in this space? They'd be watching. What would they think? I wasn't a member of their church. I was a Catholic. How would they feel if they saw me sharing a very Catholic form of devotion in their Protestant environment?

Inwardly, I rambled on like this for several minutes before once again I 'heard' Mary's voice.

Give her the silver Rosary.

In my spirit, I knew that she would not ask me again and that, if I continued to hesitate, I would risk disappointing our Holy Mother by withholding a blessing for the poor, downtrodden woman whom she was trying to comfort. I also knew that if the comfort were to be extended, Mary would need my hands to present the gift.

I had never stepped out before to share my faith. We Catholics aren't known as the 'quiet' Christians for nothing. But, in obedience, I took a deep breath, steeled myself, and took the three small steps across the aisle on shaky knees with my beloved silver Rosary in hand.

The woman's head was bent in prayer but she looked up when she felt me standing over her. For just an instant, I saw a flash of fear in her eyes. No doubt, after being refused prayer, she probably thought that I was about to ask her to leave the church.

I held out the Rosary and smiled.

"These are filled with prayers," I whispered. "I hope they give you comfort."

I'll never forget the beautiful blue eyes that stared back at me as tears ran down her weathered checks. She leaned back and cupped her hands as a Catholic would in preparation for receiving the Eucharist. I reverently slipped the strand into her hands and watched with a joyful heart as she clutched it to her breast and a gentle peace washed over her face.

A Personal Ministry Is Born

Although it greatly saddened me to relinquish my cherished Rosary, I had received a greater gift, as I remembered the enormous comfort it had provided a suffering soul.

Now that I was in need of a new Rosary, I made my way to the Catholic religious store. Gazing at the rows upon rows of colored beads, I suddenly found myself wondering if others might find similar comfort through the gift of a Rosary that had been filled with prayers said on their behalf.

Although I could not afford to give away silver Rosaries, I could afford one that was attractive, something that would be cherished. Immediately, my eyes fell across a rose-colored strand of Italian glass beads with a dogwood cross.

'What if's' filled my mind.

What if others could take comfort from a sign that God had not forgotten them?

What if Mary could use me to deliver that sign through her Rosary?

What if I were to embark on a great experiment to see if Mary would send others across my path in need of comfort?

What if I were to purchase this Rosary, pray over it and then see what developed?

I asked the salesperson to open the case and took a few moments to run the rosy beads through my hand. Perhaps Mary had foreseen, in having me present my much-cherished silver strand, that a chain of plastic beads might easily be discarded or forgotten. In my hands was a beautifully crafted piece of art that I could easily envision being cherished. The satiny glass beads and unique crucifix would become a physical reminder for someone of the intercessory prayers I had said on their behalf.

I had no idea if Mary would ever bring another person across my path, but I decided to give it try. The worst that could happen was that I would be in possession of a lovely new Rosary.

Even though the Rosary was slightly more than I had wished to spend, I told the salesperson that I would take it. I would consider the extra money spent as a tithe to the Lord.

I asked our parish priest to bless the strand, and then began my daily recitation of the Mysteries. As I prayed, I envisioned each bead filling with the power of heartfelt, intercessory prayers. Of course, I had no way of knowing if this bold experiment would work. Yet, having been so deeply touched by the reaction of the homeless lady in response to the gift, I felt in my spirit that there must be a host of others who would take comfort in holding a Rosary to their breast, knowing that it was filled with prayers said especially on their behalf. Even more profound was the knowledge that Mary had seen their suffering and had fashioned this response.

I had no real timeline. I simply prayed until I felt an inner peace that I had prayed enough prayers. Then I slipped this special Rosary into my purse, charged with a surge of excitement. I still had no idea who the Rosary was intended for or even how I would recognize that person when and *if* she or he arrived. All I knew was this: If Mary could speak to my heart once to offer my precious silver Rosary to a homeless woman knowing the comfort that the prayer-filled strand would bring, she would have no trouble doing it again.

Several weeks later, I was standing in line at the pharmacy alongside a tall, grey-haired lady smelling faintly of *Jean Nate* as we waited for a customer and the pharmacist to finish their conversation. It was evident from the exchange that there had been a mix-up in a prescription. I took a deep breath and steeled myself for a lengthy wait.

The older woman nervously glanced down at her watch. "I hope it's not going to be too much longer. My husband is home alone."

"Is your husband ill?" I asked.

She nodded. "He's in the early stages of Alzheimer's. I hate to think of what lies up ahead. I watched my father suffered from it. It's a horrible disease."

Suddenly, I felt an inner nudge as though Mary was saying, "This is the person that I have sent in need of comfort. Give her the Rosary."

Although I had anxiously anticipated this moment for weeks, now that it was here, I found myself hesitating. What if she rejected the gift, or worse, dismissed me as a religious fanatic? Then I reminded myself that I had freely embarked on this experiment by placing myself at Mary's disposal. I could hardly chicken out now.

I dug into my purse and removed the beautiful glass beads.

"These beads are filled with prayers," I said, extending the lovely rose-colored strand. "I hope it will give you comfort."

First, there was a look of shock. Then her eyes grew moist, and she cupped her hands (just as the homeless woman had done) to accept the Rosary.

"You can't imagine what this means to me. My husband has always had a great love of Mary and faithfully prayed the Rosary," she whispered, clearly overcome with emotion. "Of course with the Alzheimer's, he no longer remembers how."

She choked back tears and hugged me.

"Thank you. This is like a living message from Mary. It's as though she's saying, we're not alone. She's right there beside us."

And so began a small, personal ministry.

The Ministry of the Holy Rosary

Since that day, I have prayed over hundreds of Rosaries. Sometimes I hear the words, "Pray for peace" or renewal, faith, health, healing, reconciliation … the list is endless. As I finger each bead, I imagine infusing it with a message of hope.

Then after a time, I feel that no more prayers are necessary. I slip the strand inside my purse and wait until someone comes across my path and I feel the now familiar *push*. I remove the Rosary and slip it into cupped hands.

"These beads are full of prayers," I tell them. "I hope they give you comfort."

Each time the response is the same, whether the person is Catholic, Protestant, Jew, even atheist … it doesn't matter. They reverently accept the beads, their eyes flush with tears.

Quite often stories filter back. This person found healing. Another reconciliation. Another new spiritual depth. Another a true miracle. Some elect to keep the Rosary, but most pass it on. New stories surface.

Recently, with priestly counsel, I have answered the call to share this ministry with the others. I've called it the *'Ministry of the Holy Rosary.'* I hope that after you have read this book, you too might be encouraged to take up this powerful outreach ministry of intercessory prayer and help widen the circle of a Mother's love to those in need of comfort and hope. ॐ

Chapter 2

The Ministry of the Holy Rosary Is …

– *A light that illuminates the path to God's grace*

ॐ

Since that first Rosary I presented to a homeless woman, the Ministry of the Holy Rosary has become a precious form of sharing God's grace. Time and time again, I have seen the power of this incredible devotion to transform lives.

When a Rosary is offered and recipients learn that it has been filled with prayers said on their behalf, the look of amazement in their eyes is precious. The silent message is clear. This meeting was not by chance but by Divine appointment. Mary knows all about their troubles and has sent a messenger to deliver the physical proof of her Son's great, abiding love through the proffered Rosary.

For those recipients, this strand of beads represents a vessel of light, illuminating God's love through the dark night of the soul—those times when heartbreak threatens to choke all vestiges of faith; when the winds of adversity are so strong that one struggles to remain standing against an onslaught of doubts that make us question God's love.

We ask …

How could a loving God have allowed this great tragedy to happen when He had the power to prevent this dreaded disease, this severed relationship, this financial loss, this broken marriage vow, this untimely death?

Few have suffered the depth of sorrow experienced by the Blessed Mother, who watched her beloved Son die the cruelest of deaths; yet in the midst of those long, agonizing hours, never once did she question God or cry out, pleading for His intervention. Instead, she internalized her pain, electing to trust in the Father's sovereign plan.

Mary has never forgotten that pain or the depth of that sorrow. She carries it close to her heart. She understands intimately the fear, the arrows of unbelief aimed at those who are asked to endure life's hardships.

And so she extends her love and support through this special Rosary, the most powerful of all intercessory prayers, that has been prayed over for someone in need of a new revelation of God's enduring love—a Rosary that will help him or her find the strength and faith to rise above life's storms.

A Child in Need of a Miracle and a Mother in Need of Hope

In 2006, our daughter Heather was pregnant with her first child and I, like most crazed soon-to-be-grandmothers, seemed incapable of passing any baby-related store or store aisle without picking up a little something for my new grandson.

One day, while my daughter and I were browsing through the baby aisles at our local Wal-Mart, an older woman approached her, seeking advice on a gift needed for a baby shower her church-women's group was giving.

"I haven't shopped for infants since my oldest grandson was born and he's in college," she said. "I have no idea what today's new mother might need."

"Why don't we begin with the necessities," Heather suggested and pointed to a row of onesies. "Let's start with these."

As we searched for just the right gifts, the woman began to share the tragic story surrounding the expectant family, whose five-year-old son David had been diagnosed with acute leukemia. He had recently been admitted to an out-of-state facility that specialized in children's cancers.

"His dad is with him," the woman explained. "But his mother, Irene,* has been forbidden to fly by her doctors until the baby is born."

We discussed how hard that must be on the mother, how terrible to be separated from a desperately ill child.

Then in one of those now familiar moments, I felt a *push.* Without hesitation I reached inside my purse and pulled out the Rosary.

"Please give this to Irene," I said, extending the beads. "Tell her that they're filled with prayers and that I hope it gives her comfort during this difficult time."

The woman asked for my name and phone number and promised to pass the Rosary along.

A few days later, Irene called. She thanked me for the gift and said that the first thing she planned to do when she was reunited with David was to pin it onto his pillow.

"How is he doing?" I asked.

"Not well," was her answer, followed by a heavy pause.

I have changed the names of all the recipients throughout this story and in the ones that follow in respect for their privacy.

"Tell me about David," I prompted.

Her voice lightened as she described a happy, sweet boy who had loved to watch baseball with his dad and romp with the family dog—a hundred-pound mongrel that David insisted on calling Speed-Bump, after the child's ill-fated attempt to walk over the dog as he lay stretched out across the living room floor. Then, six months ago, the child who could devour an entire pizza at one sitting suddenly showed an indifference to food.

"Getting any food down him was a chore."

A rash of new symptoms followed—unexplained fevers, night sweats, headaches.

Then one night David awoke in severe pain. His stomach had swelled to three times its normal size. He was rushed to the emergency room. Doctors diagnosed an enlarged spleen. More tests followed and then the devastating news: David had acute leukemia.

I sensed Irene struggling to hold back tears as she shared the gravity of David's current condition and how hard it was to be separated from her son at a time when he needed her most.

"I can only bear it knowing that this hospital has one of the most progressive treatment programs in the country for tackling his form of cancer."

It was their last hope.

We spoke for several more minutes. I offered my continued prayers. Toward the end of our conversation, Irene thanked me for the Rosary.

"It's brought me so much comfort," she said. "Whenever I begin to loose hope, I take it into my hands and pray. After I say one or two decades, the fear begins to ebb and I feel a gentle peace. I'm able to cope again."

During the next six months, Irene called several times. She had since delivered a healthy, eight-pound boy and was now reunited with David. She told me how, on their first visit, she had given him such a huge hug that David joked that it was cutting off his oxygen supply. Then, she had removed the Rosary from her pocket and pinned it to his pillow as she had promised.

During the conversations that followed, Irene always began with an update on David's condition. He had a bone transplant, and a few weeks later it looked as though things had taken a turn for the better.

"Maybe the Rosary has a special blessing attached to it," she said with enormous hope. And, for a time, it looked as though it might be so. David's white count was down. He had regained some of his energy. There was even talk about bringing him home in a few weeks.

On Christmas Eve day, Paul and I were driving to a bookstore to pick up a last-minute gift when my cellphone rang. It was Irene. David had slipped into a coma. The transplant had failed. They had run out of options. It was just a matter of hours before he would slip away.

There was little that I could do but listen, my heart breaking for this dear woman.

Through heavy sobs, she asked the same questions others had asked during times of great trials. Where was God in all of this? How could He allow a small, innocent child, who had done nothing to warrant this, to suffer and die?

Since I had lost a three-year-old granddaughter in a tragic accident, I was able to offer some comfort. I, too, had asked the same questions. My granddaughter was so young, so full of life and promise. Why couldn't God have intervened on my behalf?

I offered what comfort I could. We prayed for God's peace and that the angels of the Lord would gather this tender young soul and deliver it safely into the Father's arms. David died that night.

It was several months before I spoke with Irene again. I asked her how she was coping. She said it had been rough in the beginning. Everything reminded her of her dear boy. For a time, she had thoughts of suicide. Anything to end the pain. But then she would glance into the crib of her newborn son and know that she must go on.

Toward the end of our conversation, she said something that would fuel this Ministry of the Holy Rosary during times when I questioned its importance:

"When I'm about to give in to despair and doubt and anger, I pick up the Rosary and begin to recite the Mysteries. It reminds me that if my faith is more than just lip service … if I truly believe its tenets … then I can't despair when suffering comes to call. And even though I don't understand why God would allow my sweet son to undergo such pain and die, the Rosary makes me focus on the example of Mary, who bravely answered God's call even though it was to bring her unimaginable suffering. I can only pray that God will use my suffering to ease the pain of others who must endure what I've endured."

I never heard from Irene again, but it is my belief that she has become a Cross Bearer—like Simeon who had been pulled from the crowd to help Jesus carry his cross—she now helps others as they make their way along their own Via Dolorosa with Mary prayerfully at their side. ℘

Chapter 3

The Ministry of the Holy Rosary Is ...

– *A vessel for the conversion of souls*

ॐ

In the parable of the lost sheep, Jesus speaks of the Father's great love, a love so deep that He would do all in His power to assure that none would perish ...

"If a man owns a hundred sheep and one of them wanders away, will he not leave the ninety-nine on the hills and go to look for the one that wandered off? And if he finds it, I tell you the truth, he is happier about that one sheep than about the ninety-nine that did not wander off. In the same way, your Father in heaven is not willing that any of these little ones should be lost."

Matthew 18:12-14

Most priests would admit that the one area in which Catholics fall short is evangelizing their faith. For many, even the term 'evangelizing' is distasteful, conjuring up images of street-corner preachers and religious fanatics who use the scare tactics of 'repent or be damned' to preach the message of salvation.

But Mary has a gentler way of gathering in the lost sheep. Through this intercessory devotional, she provides a wonderful opportunity to embrace the souls who are at risk of eternal separation from the Father. Not with words of condemnation or loud proclamations, but through an outstretched hand in time of need into which a special Rosary—filled with prayers on their behalf—is placed.

Redemption Brought to a Troubled Teen

One of the saddest facets of our culture is the obsessive focus on beauty. In today's secular world, the body has become society's golden calf.

Seldom can we turn on a television show or pick up a magazine that doesn't highlight how we might adorn our body, groom it, pump it up, or change its shape. Our bathroom shelves are stockpiled with a host of elixirs promising to reduce wrinkles, plump up thinning eyelashes, firm sagging chins, and revitalize lackluster skin.

These messages of imperfection are especially blaring for teenage girls. Magazines that cater to today's youth are filled with photos of reed-thin models who look more like walking cadavers than like young women with the robust bodies that God intended them to have. Fashion models, who have become the holy icon of many teens, now average a size 0, with a 23-inch waist and 30-inch hips.

As completely unrealistic as these measurements are, many teenage girls are literally starving themselves in order to fit the media's interpretation of what is fashionably chic. Forget that we are made in God's image, and that in God's eyes thinness does not matter. In today's teenage culture, it matters a lot.

Alarmingly, a recent look at the current statistics shows that 42 percent of first- to third-grade girls want to be thinner. Some 81 percent of 10 year-olds are afraid of being fat. And 51 percent of 9- and 10-year-old girls feel better about themselves if they are on a diet. These are *children* who should be enjoying things like popcorn and movie nights with their family and friends, or taking part in the inter-active sports in school, or joining the Church youth group, not angst-ing over the calorie count of a piece of lettuce. Because of this weight obsession, serious eating disorders have nearly doubled in the last decade. Of those who are not treated, 20 percent will die.

So when my relative Debra called with the devastating news that her 16-year-old daughter Loren had just been hospitalized with an advanced case of anorexia, I was deeply concerned.

Debra is one of the most kind, generous and endearing people that I know. I love her dearly, and it grieves me deeply that she feels religion is unnecessary and that she left the Catholic faith during her college years. As I listened to the details of Loren's condition, I yearned to offer comfort, but knew that Debra would dismiss any mention of prayer or faith in God's ability to heal.

Although we differ greatly on our beliefs, I respect her right to believe as she chooses. That does not mean, however, that I have abandoned storming the gates of Heaven in her behalf, so that she might someday be restored to the Church and the fullness of the Sacraments. Still, I was greatly saddened that, in a time of such intense anguish, I could not offer her the greatest comfort of all—the steadfastness of our faith under fire.

The coming days were filled with deep concern as Loren's weight plummeted to 68 pounds, which necessitated her being strapped to a hospital bed. At this point, even the slightest movement would expend calories that would put her internal organs at risk of shutting down. I could only imagine Debra's torment for her beloved daughter.

I had recently purchased a lovely strand of Rosaries. Made of hand-blown glass, they were the pale pink of a summer sunrise. I dedicated the Rosary to Loren and began immediately to infuse the beads with prayers on her behalf. Every time I prayed, I envisioned this sweet, gentle teen growing healthy and strong; but mostly, finding the peace that comes through the knowledge that she was a beloved child of God.

It was touch and go for several weeks, but slowly, Loren began to improve. She was moved to a facility that dealt exclusively with weight disorders. The program was very structured and tightly monitored. Cellphones and computers were forbidden.

During those long, difficult months, I sent packages, cards and little trinkets that I thought she might enjoy or that could help to pass the time. With each, I enclosed a card with the words, "I'm praying for you."

Following the receipt of each gift, Loren would send a thank-you card with a short note on her progress or a description of the programs that she was attending. Then one day, I noted the phrase posted at the end of her note, "And I'm praying, too."

Those four short words filled me with great hope. Here was a child who had never been introduced to prayer; yet I believed that, with Mary's intervention through the Rosary, Loren was finding her way to God.

Over the next two years, Loren was in and out of facilities. I'd get a frantic call from Debra. Loren's weight had plummeted once again. My heart nearly broke with each relapse. I'd hurriedly called prayerful friends, added her name to prayer chains and asked Mary to hold her close.

Meanwhile, there were family counseling sessions; group meetings where other girls victimized by this horrid disease gathered to share their struggles; private counseling, and endless therapy sessions to help refashion negative thoughts surrounding food consumption.

In my spirit, however, I knew that what Loren needed most was to be touched by the "Great Physician." Only His peace could recondition her troubled mind. But out of respect for Debra's feelings about the Church, I kept these thoughts to myself, electing instead to step up the Rosary, filling it with prayers for healing, renewal and redemption.

Another episode. Another rush to the hospital. Another vigil. But this time when Debra called, I found the courage to ask if I might send Loren the Rosary that I had been praying over. To my delight, she said yes. I boxed it up and sent it along that very day.

Then an amazing thing began to happen. The episodes grew less frequent. Loren was still very ill, but the peaks and valleys began to level out. I continued to write, encouraging her to pray the Rosary and asking Mary to help her find peace and healing. And with each letter, I added, "I'm praying for you" to which she always replied, "And I'm praying, too."

Then one day, I opened my e-mail to find a letter from Debra saying that Loren had contacted the local Catholic Church and was now meeting with the pastor once a week to explore the tenets of our Catholic faith. Six months later, Loren entered the Rite of Christian Initiation (RCIA) which is the process through which adults and older children are prepared to enter into the fullness of the Sacraments of the Roman Catholic Church. I'm happy to report that I was chosen to be one of her co-sponsors. That coming Easter, she was brought into the fullness of the Church.

Loren continues to have ups and downs but is braving it through. She recently entered college and joined a sorority. Although this disease will always be a challenge to contain, she now has the support of our faith community, the prayers of the saints, the powerful healing inherent in the Eucharist and our Blessed Mother's kind embrace signified by the Rosary that dear Loren now clutches in her hand. ⬍

Chapter 4

The Ministry of the Holy Rosary Is ...

– *A vessel used to comfort the dying*

ॐ

All men must die, an irrefutable statement that most of us find far too difficult to contemplate. We push this sober fact to the far recesses of our mind, preferring to say with Scarlet O'Hara ... *I'll think about it tomorrow.*

Thoughts of death are especially hard for the young to contemplate. Life stretches out before them. The world is their playground. Youth is a time to focus on happier matters. Finding the right job. The perfect mate to share one's life followed by the dreams that young couples have—the planning of the wedding, buying a home, anticipating the birth of the first child.

But sometimes fate steps in and curtails these plans. We walk into a doctor's office to receive test results for what we assumed had been a minor complaint and leave with a diagnosis that a deadly cancer is eating away at our organs. Suddenly, without warning, we are facing the stark reality of our mortality.

Elizabeth Kubler Ross wrote extensively about death and dying, listing the six phases of grief that people experience as they wrestle with their approaching death.

First, there is denial. The medical report can't be correct. The doctors or lab technicians must have made a mistake.

The second is anger. We're too young to die. We're not finished with all the things we wished to accomplish. We rail against the injustice of this sudden shift in fate. How can we be dying when others—murders, terrorists, child molesters, those who openly practice corporate greed—are allowed to go on?

Bargaining follows, a vain expression of hope that the outcome can somehow be re-negotiated. What if we promise to change our lifestyle? Care for our body more, with better diet and exercise? What if we are more compassionate and open to the needs of others? What if we help others, maybe volunteering at a hospital? Perhaps through these acts we might make ourselves indispensible to God and He will let us live.

When bargaining does not work, we fall into a state of deep depression. The inevitability of our fate has sunk in. We internalize our fear and pain by pulling away from the help extended by caregivers and family. We conclude that our situation is hopeless and that there is no reason to rail against what can't be changed.

During the fifth stage, we decide that we can no longer remain in this state of despair, and we slowly begin to surface from the dark hole. Dying, we now welcome loved ones as we seek ways to retain whatever control we can at this point, such as new treatments or medicines to help curb the pain.

Six and the last phase in preparing for death is acceptance. No amount of fighting or pleading will change the outcome. We go from passive to active participant in working through the last phase of life. During this phase, the emphasis often shifts from us to those who will be left behind. We might put our estate in order; make funeral plans and begin to prepare our loved ones for this final passage.

Sadly, many family members are often unable to accept their loved one's impending death, going to great lengths to avoid talking about the subject or insisting that the dying will somehow 'beat this thing.'

There's nothing quite as sad as watching the dying being forced to bottle up their need to express their last thoughts in deference to their loved ones' refusal to accept the inevitable.

A Last Wish

To my great surprise, my dear husband Paul presented me with an exact replica of the silver Rosary that I had given to the homeless woman. This time, however, I was making certain that it stayed in my nightstand drawer. At least that was *my* plan. Our Blessed Mother, however, had another.

One day, as I was getting ready to begin my intercessory prayers, I felt a strong need to pray over the silver Rosary as I had with other strands that Mary had earmarked to be given away. Then, in the innermost part of my soul, I heard Mary's voice. *Pray for healing.*

I glanced down at the beautiful silver Rosary and thought, "You're kidding, right?" She couldn't *really* be asking me to prepare another silver Rosary to be given away. I reasoned that it must be some kind of test. Maybe she just wanted to make certain that I would be obedient to her requests.

While I did as instructed, I was careful to keep all this from Paul. How could I possibly tell him that this beautiful, cherished Rosary might also have been earmarked by Mary?

I descended to subterfuge. During devotions, I kept another Rosary on hand just in case Paul might happen into the room while I was praying.

I prayed steadily over the silver Rosary for several weeks, then felt that no additional prayers were needed. Quickly, I got busy preparing another strand in hopes that Mary might allow me to substitute it for the silver one now tucked inside my purse.

Then one day, I received a call from a woman who identified herself as Mindy. She had heard that my art studio offered classes and wondered if I was accepting new students. I told her that there was an opening in my Thursday night class, and she asked if she might bring her sister, Joan. She explained that Joan was suffering from liver cancer.

"She has always wanted to learn to paint, and I thought that art lessons might help to get her mind off all that she's going through. But you should know that she tires easily."

I explained that students were encouraged to go at their own pace. Then, sensing that Mindy might be concerned that Joan's condition could disrupt the class, I quickly added that she would be with other students who had been diagnosed with cancer.

"Art is a wonderful way to give expression to the inner turmoil that cancer patients experience," I said, having had several such patients attend my classes down through the years. "In fact, she might enjoy the opportunity to speak with others who have experienced what she is going through."

"May I stay?" Mindy asked, quickly adding, "Just in case she needs to leave early."

I assured her that would be fine, although I felt Mindy's real concerns had more to do with leaving her sister in the care of strangers.

For the next six weeks, Joan and Mindy were regulars. Although frail, Joan had a wonderful outlook and sunny smile that quickly endeared her to the other students. Since relatives of cancer patients often treat them like delicate porcelain, this was a safe haven, a place where they could rip it up and laugh … yes … laugh … at the indignities and in some cases, their approaching death.

In my studio, no holds were barred. They shared jokes about the unfairness of this disease that robbed them of their lovely locks of hair, yet left hair on their legs that they still had to shave, One, an elderly woman, joked about when, as she went through the rigors of chemotherapy for breast cancer, her physician suggested that she smoke a little pot for the nausea. The image of this grandmotherly woman trying to purchase 'weed' from a street vendor had us in stitches.

Joan joined right in, sparring with the best of them. I did, however, note that most of her jokes centered on death and dying. Mindy appeared especially uncomfortable during these repartees. It was clear by her body language and her repeated comments that "Joan would outlive them all" that it was an unwelcome subject.

Over the next few weeks, Joan's condition began to rapidly deteriorate until it was impossible for her to continue. She stopped coming to class. Meanwhile, I felt a strong urge to offer her the silver Rosary, whose choice now made great sense. Possessed of an artist's heart, Joan would greatly appreciate the beauty and craftsmanship of this lovely Rosary.

A few weeks later, I received a call from Mindy. She asked if I would pray for Joan, who was nearing the end of her battle. I asked if I might offer Joan a Rosary that had been filled with prayers on her behalf. I did not mention that those prayers had been for healing, since Mary had been very specific about the type of prayers that should be offered through this intercessory strand of beads. Did that mean that I doubted that divine healing was possible? No. I did, however, constantly question my right to share private insights with others. If a healing were available for Joan, then that would be made evident without any prophesying on my part.

Toward the end of the call, I asked if she might like to host a prayer gathering of friends and family. Mindy eagerly agreed and I instructed that each participant be asked to fast and pray for three days before the gathering, since I had found this to be the most effective.

I'll never forget the scene that day. It was one of the most beautiful prayer gatherings I have ever attended. A great crowd had gathered as dusk cast a soft golden glow over the gardens that stretched along the borders of Mindy's backyard. We formed a circle around Joan, who was seated in a wicker chair.

Even though the earth still pulsated with the heat of a mid-summer sun, she was wrapped in a woolen shawl. Her weight had plummeted since I had last seen her. She was now literally just skin and bones. But no one could have mistaken the inner glow and vibrant joy that resonated on her face as she surveyed the crowd. She was encased in a circle of love.

First we began collectively to ask God to shed His grace and mercy on Joan and her family. Familiar prayers followed—the Hail Mary, Our Father—slowly rising like incense as each joined in. Some prayed with uplifted faces. Others with eyes closed, lips moving silently as they earnestly petitioned the Father on Joan's behalf.

Someone lifted up the first verse of "Amazing Grace." All followed as tears flowed and hands were raised in supplication.

Then, one by one, each stepped forward to place a hand on Joan's shoulder and pray a personal heartfelt prayer on her behalf. I can confidently say that there wasn't a single person who was not deeply touched that day.

A buffet supper signified the end of our three-day fast. When the prayers ended, we gathered around several large folding tables nearly bursting with food. Joan's family was Italian. Need I say more? The tables groaned under platters of eggplant parmesan, lasagna, chicken cacciatore, veal Marsala, sausage and peppers, antipastos, bowls of salads with savory dressings and enough desserts to fill a small bakery.

At one point, I happened to glance over at Joan. She was smiling broadly, surrounded by her two sisters and a brother, the silver Rosary draped over her lap. For the first time in weeks, she was eating and appeared to be relishing each bite. I remembered Mary's prompting to pray for healing and I felt a surge of hope. Could these prayers have actually affected a cure? For days afterward, I continued to intercede on Joan's behalf, reminding myself that the age of miracles had not passed. But there would be no miracle for Joan. Two weeks later, Mindy called. Joan had died in her arms that morning.

I was devastated for this close-knit family, but I was also filled with uncertainties about the ministry. I had heard Mary instruct me to pray for healing, yet Joan had died. My faith was greatly shaken.

If I had gotten that wrong, how could I trust what I would receive in the future? The excitement I first experienced with this ministry came to a crashing halt. I was suddenly plagued with doubts.

I sought counsel from a dear priest friend. He quietly allowed me to vent my confusion. Finally, spent, he leaned forward and assured me that he saw nothing wrong with what I was doing. In fact, he had encouraged me from the beginning. Still, he advised me to set the ministry aside for a time.

"When in doubt, wait. If Mary wishes you to continue, she'll bring you the understanding you seek."

A month later, I received a letter from Mindy. Enclosed was the silver Rosary. The first few lines expressed the family's appreciation for all I had done. Then she wrote …

"You'll never know the healing that took place that night."

My pulse quickened at the reference to healing. I eagerly read on.

"Up until that night, we had refused to believe that Joan might die. Instead, we rejected any mention of death. But that night after we had prayed, we allowed Joan to talk about her death. She expressed how in the beginning she was fearful, but now, she was at peace. She was especially eager to see our parents again.

"It was clear how much she needed to share her feelings and how our silence had pained her all these past months. She needed to talk about her impending death. She needed for us to 'hear' her last wishes.

"For my family and myself, I wish to thank you. That night brought us all together in this final chapter of Joan's life."

A New Commitment

When I began to pray over that Rosary, I had heard 'healing' and just assumed that Mary meant a physical healing. But she had meant something much more profound.

The healing that was brought to Joan was one that removed her feelings of isolation and rejoined her with her family. Through their acceptance of her imminent death, Joan found renewed faith that allowed her to die peacefully with the full assurance that through prayer and God's grace nothing could ever truly separate her from the family she was leaving behind. ॐ

Chapter 5

The Ministry of the Holy Rosary Is ...

– *A vessel as a channel of healing*

ॐ

In March, 2009 in Cleveland, Ohio, 26-year-old Jory Aebly, a hospital lab technician, and a friend were forced into a city park, robbed, then made to kneel while a 17-year-old gunman shot them both through the head execution style.

The friend was pronounced dead at the scene, while Jory was rushed to Metro Medical Center in critical condition. The bullet had pierced both hemispheres of the brain leaving a trail of fragments. When his family arrived, doctors offered them little hope, stating that Jory's injuries were non-survivable. The doctors, however, did not factor in the power of the Rosary. Enter Father Art Snedeker, hospital chaplain at Metro Medical Center.

Called to perform the Sacrament of the Sick, Father Snedeker entrusted the young man to the intercession of Pope John Paul II and placed a Rosary that had been blessed by the Pontiff on the boy's bed.

Years ago, the priest had been given a private audience with Pope John Paul II. They shared a mutual friend, a physician attached to the Metro Medical Center. At the end of the session, Father Snedeker asked if the Pope would bless the 12 Rosaries that he had brought along. The last of these strands was given to Jory.

To the amazement of Jory's neurosurgeon, Dr. Robert Geertman, the young man did not die. Instead, he continued to improve and, within three weeks of the near-fatal shooting, walked with the aid of a walker. Five weeks later (which coincidentally was just two days short of the fourth anniversary of Pope John Paul II's death), Jory Aebly was released to go home. Dr. Robert Geertman called his recovery "One in a million."

There was another reported instance of healing attributable to God's intervention through the Rosary. Rita Klaus, of Pittsburgh, Pennsylvania, a teacher and a mother of three, had suffered from Multiple Sclerosis for 26 years. One day after reading about the Marian apparitions in Medjugorje, Yugoslavia, she decided to pray the Rosary for healing. While in prayer, she said she felt a gentle warmth and a quiet assurance that her prayer had been answered. She had been healed. Later, doctors who referred to her previous medical records affirmed that Klaus had indeed suffered from MS; they said that there was no medical explanation for her complete healing.

Miracles attributable to the Rosary are numerous. Father Patrick Peyton, known as the "Rosary Priest" for his deep devotion to Mary and the family Rosary, attributed the prayers of the Rosary for his healing of tuberculosis.

A Woman in Need of a Miracle

During the 1990's, the condo that my husband and I were renting was put up for sale. The landlord had recently died and his son wished to settle the estate. The son asked if we would allow a realtor to view the unit. We agreed and made an early-morning appointment.

The realtor arrived at the agreed-upon time with a co-worker whom she introduced as Jane. She explained that Jane couldn't stay but would take a cursory tour, then had to dash to drive her husband to an early-morning medical appointment.

While the realtor and I chatted, Jane inspected the main floor then headed upstairs to the bedrooms and my office. Minutes later, she called down from the upstairs balcony.

"I saw one of your manuscripts lying on your desk. You're Katherine Valentine."

I said that I was.

"I can't believe that God led me here this morning!" she shouted, bounding down the stairs to give me a huge hug while her co-worker looked on with confusion.

"I kept an article that was written about you a few years back," she said. "It spoke about your spiritual journey after God miraculously cured you of cancer."

I remembered the article, although I had since shied away from talking about the healing. I had grown increasingly uncomfortable as people sought me out as some kind of sage, insistent that I must have a direct line to God's grace even though I made it very clear that I was just like everyone else, with more questions than answers.

"I've referred to that article dozens of times since my husband was diagnosed with brain tumors." Her eyes grew misty. "He's scheduled for surgery tomorrow. I'm taking him for a series of final tests this morning."

I had just finished praying over a Rosary that morning and still had it in my sweater pocket. I handed it over to Jane.

"These are filled with prayers," I said. "I hope they give you comfort."

Clutching the strand in her hand, she fought to retain control as she whispered, "I have to go." Then she fled out the front door.

The next day, Jane appeared at our home, carrying a large bouquet of red roses with a face wreathed in smiles.

"These are for you," she said, extending the flowers.

"For me? But why?"

"I gave the Rosary to my husband when I went to picked him up for his pre-surgical appointment. He kept it with him while they did a battery of tests."

"And?" I could feel the excitement mounting.

"We just finished speaking with the doctors. There's no longer any evidence of tumors."

We were both crying as she handed me the Rosary. "I wanted to return this in case someone else might need it."

I folded the strand back into her hand and said, "Pass it on."

Father Joe's Rosary

Down through the years, I have been greatly blessed to be surrounded by wonderful priests, men who are true shepherds and whose love and compassion for their flock mirrors Christ. Father Joe Keough is one such priest.

We met in the 90's when he arrived at my parish to assist our aging pastor. He had worked in marketing for several years before accepting the call to the priesthood, so he had a deep understanding of how hard it is to maintain one's faith in an everyday world. He was also part of a loving family whose antics, especially those of his nephews, kept him well supplied with fodder for his Sunday homilies. When Father Joe left to co-pastor another parish, I gave him a Rosary that I had prayed over especially for his intentions.

I knew that his next parish would greatly benefit from his special gifts.

The sex scandal was just beginning to rock the Church and sadly, many of my priest friends had stopped wearing their collars in public for fear of harassment. At the time, it seemed that the media had launched a campaign to cast all priests as suspects and the Church as a house of shame.

Granted that the crimes—and they were crimes—committed by this handful of priests were odious. But in no way did these men represent the shepherds that I knew, priests who cherished their vows and lived lives that truly represented the Lord's call for compassion, mercy and love.

I fondly remember one priest who had been an engineer before his priesthood. His parish was largely comprised of immigrants who lived in sub-standard tenement buildings owned by indifferent landlords. Several times throughout the winter, one of the furnaces would go out. The tenants knew it was useless to call the landlord, so they would call their favorite priest to come and get it going again.

One particular cold, wintry night, the priest was just finishing up repairs, when he noticed that the man who had volunteered to assist him was standing barefoot on the cold, cement basement floor. He told him to run upstairs and fetch his pair of shoes. He would finish up without him.

The man lowered his head, his face red with shame as he confessed that he didn't own a pair. He and another man, who worked nights, shared a single pair of boots. Without hesitation, the priest removed his boots and handed them over to the man. The man protested, but the priest insisted, even though it meant walking barefooted back to the rectory through the snow-covered city streets.

These are the kinds of priests that I know. They are seldom noted by the media.

One morning, I received an e-mail from Father Joe Keough, asking if I would pray for a parishioner. His name was Alex, and he was a high-school freshman who had just been admitted to intensive care.

That morning, Alex had been hit by a car while jogging. He suffered severe internal injuries and was on life support. His prognosis was very poor.

I wrote back to assure Father that I would hold Alex up in my prayers and suggested that he take Alex the Rosary that I had given him.

Father Joe later wrote back.

"I placed the Rosary on Alex's forehead and prayed with his parents. Alex soon stabilized and doctors say he'll make a complete recovery."

Today, this young man is attending college, where he is majoring in Philosophy. Father Joe even reports that Alex may have a vocation as a priest. ॐ

Chapter 6

The Ministry of the Holy Rosary Is ...

– *A vessel of hope for all faiths*

ॐ

From the very beginning of this ministry, Mary pressed upon my heart that she is the Universal Mother to *all* of mankind. Catholic, Protestant, Jew, Muslim, Hindu or any other faith, Mary embraces them all as their Blessed Mother. This is especially true for those who suffer. And, through her tender mercies, our Mother gently leads them to her beloved Son.

Numerous times over the years, I have felt the familiar *push* to offer a Rosary to a Protestant or a non-Christian. One particular incident stands out in my mind.

I was on my way to the library to return a book when an elderly couple flagged me down as I was about to enter the building.

"My husband and I have missed our bus back to the village and need a ride home," the small, grey-haired lady told me. Seated beside her on a stone bench was her husband, looking extremely frail.

The 'village' she referred to is a large retirement complex in town that consists of some 2,700 senior condominiums. A private bus service ferries the occupants to and from various points in the community; but, if residents miss their ride back, they're expected to make their own way home.

"Would you happen to be going past there?" she asked with a slight hint of urgency.

"Just let me run these books inside, and I'll be happy to give you a ride," I said, knowing that even if I had no intention of going their way, I couldn't in good conscience leave them stranded.

"Oh, thank you, dear," she said, her strained face flooding with relief. "We're the Rosenbergs. I'm Ruth and this is my husband, Morty. He isn't feeling well and I really do need to get him home."

I hurried inside the library, deposited my books, then scurried back and directed the Rosenbergs to my car. That year, I was teaching a fifth grade CCD class and my mini-van was filled with workbooks, religious cards and bags of plastic Rosaries. I hastily moved everything aside as the old gentleman slid into the front passenger seat and his wife got into the back.

As I started the car, Morty studied the small bags of plastic rosaries scattered along the dashboard.

"I hope you don't plan on talking to me about religion," he snapped, nodding toward the Rosaries. "I don't believe in religion."

I stifled a smile. The old curmudgeon. Talk about *chutzpah*.

"I can assure you that it was not my intention to talk about religion," I said, deciding to ignore his rude behavior. The man was old. He was obviously ill.

I went on to explain that I taught religious education for my parish and hadn't had time to clean out my car. I refrained from adding ... not that I should have to clean it out just in case I was hailed down by a stranded, anti-religious senior citizen.

"Now, Morty," his wife placated. "She was kind enough to give us a ride home. Don't go making trouble."

"Trouble? Who's making trouble? I'm just saying a ride we need. Religion we don't," he said, folding his arms as if to seal the matter.

I prayed for patience and remembered the saying, "Difficult people aren't the problem. They're the lesson." Then I wondered what lesson Morty had come to deliver.

It was a short ride to the village and, within 10 minutes, we were drawing close to their home. It was then that Morty turned and asked, "So, you believe in all this stuff, huh?"

I donned my best smile. "If what you mean by 'stuff' is God and the power of faith, yes I believe in it."

"What part of it?" he challenged.

"All of it," I answered.

I glanced in the rear view mirror and saw Ruth's face tighten. She leaned forward and patted her husband's shoulder. "Now, Morty …"

"What?" he shrugged. "Can't I talk?"

Ruth sighed and settled back against her seat.

"So, I suppose this faith of yours, it should believe that God answers prayer."

I nodded.

"Which prayers?"

For a man who didn't want to talk about religion, he seemed very interested.

"Every prayer," I said.

"Humph!" He turned to look out his side window.

For the last moments of the ride, Morty remained quiet; yet in my spirit I sensed that he was not as anti-religious as he had claimed. In fact, I sensed that there was a war going on inside this old man's soul.

I pulled up to their cluster of condos, which was perched on the edge of a hill and afforded an uninterrupted view of the valley below. It was breathtaking, yet the pair hardly glanced at its beauty as I helped them out of the van. Ruth flitted around nervously as she tried to help Morty out of the car while he kept slapping her hand away.

I asked if they needed assistance to their home, but Ruth declined. "You've done quite enough already, dear."

"Then I'll be going," I said and turned to leave.

"Wait," Morty said, then addressed his wife. "I want her praying for me tomorrow. Get her phone number."

"You want me to pray for you?" Wasn't this the same man who had begun our ride with a 'don't talk to me about religion'?

"My husband is going in for a triple bypass," Ruth hastened to explain. "The doctor said that … well …"

"That I might not make it," Morty finished.

Now I understood his belligerence and why he had lashed out against religion. His Jewish faith did not offer the comfort of the immortality of our Risen Lord. I believe that for Morty, death meant an end, not a beginning.

Suddenly, I saw this small, shriveled man through the eyes of Christ—Morty's fears, his need to be comforted. Then I felt the familiar *push,* and although it seemed unlikely that he would be receptive to a symbol of Christian prayer, I obeyed.

I dug into my pocket and removed the Rosary while trusting the Holy Spirit to provide just the right words. I handed Morty the strand of beads.

"This Rosary is filled with many prayers offered through a Jewish Mother who knows a great deal about suffering," I told him.

"If it gives you comfort, I would like to offer it to you with the assurance that both of us will be praying for you tomorrow."

He clutched the Rosary as though it was a lifeline and brusquely turned before I could see the tears as I gave Ruth my phone number.

As promised, I spent a good portion of my early-morning prayer time in intercession for Morty. I prayed that the operating room would be filled with angels and songs of praise that would bring him peace. That the surgeon hands would be divinely guided and that the medical staff would be given extraordinary skills. Then, as the Bible quotes, *"Having done all, stand."* I left the outcome in God's hand and began my day at the computer, working on editor's notes for my newest novel.

Mid-afternoon the phone rang. Normally when I'm writing, I let the answering machine pick up but, sensing that it might be Ruth, I reached for the phone.

"Kate? This is Ruth," she began. Immediately, I could sense relief in her voice. "Dr. Filene just called. Morty's going to be fine. In fact, he said that, for a man his age, he came through the surgery with flying colors. I wanted to thank you for your prayers."

"You're welcome."

Then she laughed. "Before Dr. Filene hung up, he said, 'I thought you and your husband were Jewish.' I told him we were. Then he asked why my husband wouldn't let them administer anesthesia until they first pinned the Rosary he was carrying to his hospital gown."

A Protestant Apostle for Mary

One of the most exciting parts about this ministry has been the many places that Mary has led me to minister to the hurt and suffering. In 2007, my husband and I found ourselves in Kentucky. The rolling hills and warm, welcoming people provided a wonderful backdrop to a ministry that seemed to be growing on its own.

During our stay I met Julia, who owned a large farm on the outskirts of town. She grew produce in the summer and pumpkins in the fall and sold Christmas trees during the holidays. The farm spanned over 100 acres and would have been an enormous undertaking for a fleet of farm workers, so I was amazed to discover that she and one farmhand worked it alone. I liked her right away. She had a gentle, kind spirit coupled with one of the most indomitable faiths that I have ever witnessed.

During that first meeting, she shared a string of sadness, beginning with the death of her step-daughter of a drug overdose four months earlier. She left behind a seven-year-old daughter, Shannon. Then, just three weeks later, Julia's husband died of a heart attack.

When I asked how she had gotten through all of it, she replied she had to keep going for her granddaughter.

"Knowing that the dear child had just lost two of the most important people in her life kept me strong," she said. "So, I made a decision right then that I wouldn't let my grief keep me from being there for her."

Then suddenly, her son-in-law Frank decided to ransom visitations rights with her granddaughter for a share in the family farm that he felt his due. The man had a prison record and Julia knew that if she agreed it would cost her the farm. She denied his requests, and Frank withheld all contact with Shannon.

"I've been praying that the Lord would help me work this out," she confided to me that day. "The longer I'm separated from her, the harder it gets to keep going."

I dug inside my purse and handed her a Rosary while I shared my story.

I told her that, shortly after a tragic accident took the life of our three-year-old granddaughter Marissa in 1994, our son stopped taking our calls. He never explained why, nor did he give us an opportunity to discuss the matter, although I felt that its core was rooted in his anger toward God. And since I was a Catholic writer and speaker, he was angry with me by association.

With sadness, Paul and I finally decided that his silence was part of the grieving process and simply backed away. For six long years, I pined for my three surviving granddaughters and prayed continuously for their return into our lives, asking our Blessed Mother to intercede on our behalf.

Then one day, a friend gave me a Rosary that had been given to her from a nun stationed at the shrine in Medjugorje.

"I feel that this Rosary is not for you," the nun told my friend. "You are to pass it along."

My friend presented it to me, and I draped the lovely strand of beads across a small stature of Madonna and child that sat on my bookcase.

My granddaughter's death date was October 2. Three years later, at two o'clock on the morning on October 2, Paul shook me awake.

"Where's that light coming from?" he asked.

Half asleep, I glanced at the beads draped across the statue. They were glowing like a 100-watt bulb.

"It's a sign from Mary," I told him excitedly. "We're going to be reunited with our granddaughters."

The first week in December, we received a letter from our son. He asked if we could forgive him for the years of silence and invited us to visit the girls.

Now, I pointed to the Rosary as I told Julia, "Mary brought my granddaughters back into my life, and I know that she will help return your granddaughter as well."

Her eyes were thick with tears as she studied the beads. "Does it matter that I'm not a Catholic?"

"Not at all," I assured her. "Mary is the Universal Mother to all and the Rosary is a powerful devotional of intercessory prayer that has no denominational boundaries."

A few months later, Julia and her granddaughter were reunited.

Through our combined suffering and love of the Lord, Julia and I became great friends. During one of our conversations, she said that she was seldom without the Rosary I had given her. She placed it beneath her pillow at night and in her purse whenever she went out. Although at this point she did not pray the Rosary, she later told me that just having it near gave her great comfort.

Although my husband and I returned to our beloved New England that winter, Julia and I have kept in touch. We talk about everything from the weather (which I've discovered is a *very* important subject to farmers), books we've read and would recommend and—since Kentucky is *the* horse state—the Equestrian Olympics being held in Lexington and the Kentucky Derby.

But mostly, we talk about grandchildren. My granddaughters are now full-fledged teenagers and have less time for their grandmother, although they do e-mail or text from time to time to catch me up on school dances and on who made the cheerleading squad. And Julia's granddaughter is busy with school choir. Sadly, from time to time, Frank decides not to allow her to see Shannon for no other reason than because he can. Julia takes up the Rosary, trusting Mary to work things out. She always does.

But mostly, we talk about matters of faith.

Recently, Julia asked if I knew anything about retreat facilities. (Is the Pope Catholic, I asked her?) It was mid-winter. The farm lay dormant under a gentle layer of snow. It was the perfect time to take a well-deserved rest.

"Do you know anything about the Abbey of Gethsemani near Bardstown?" she asked.

Paul and I had visited it several times during our stay in Kentucky. Nestled among soft, undulating hills, the Abbey is run by a group of Trappist Monks dedicated to prayer and service. They also have a deep devotion to Mary. I highly recommended it.

Julia chose a weeklong retreat. I teased this born-again Christian about having to stay in a 'cell.' When she gasped, I quickly assured her that it was just another term for a very sparse bedroom.

Julia melded right into the daily routine of contemplation and prayer. I knew she would. I've never known anyone so open to the move of the Holy Spirit. Later, she asked if I would like to read the journal that she kept those seven days. I was honored. Many of the passages moved me to tears.

While she was there, Julia made friends with a nun who offered to show her how to pray the Rosary. For the duration of Julia's stay, the two women met each evening to pray the Mysteries.

Shortly after returning home, Julia met with her lawyer, and the two women got to talking about family issues. The lawyer confided that she was going through a difficult time, one she wasn't sure could be resolved. Hearing the heartbreak in the woman's voice prompted Julia to share the story of Frank's refusal to allow her to see her granddaughter, Shannon.

"How did you work that all out?" the lawyer asked.

Julia removed the Rosary from her purse, then began to share the comfort that it had brought her during those difficult times—and the power that she had experienced through this special devotional prayer.

"I don't know a lot about the Rosary. I'm still learning," my born-again Christian friend confessed to her Protestant lawyer. "But maybe you should try praying it."

The lawyer leaned forward and studied the outstretched strand of beads, thought a moment then said, "Maybe I should."

Julia purchased another Rosary and later delivered it to the lawyer's office. She called me that same day, filled with excitement over how it was received. "She came out from around her desk and gave me a big hug. We both got misty-eyed."

Julia has since purchased other strands of beads.

"I know there are a lot more hurting people out there," she says. "And I want to be prepared when Mary sends them my way." ❧

Chapter 7

The Ministry of the Holy Rosary Is ...

– People joining together in intercessory prayer

ॐ

Several years ago (before the cellphone era) my car stalled in the middle of Asylum Avenue in Hartford, Connecticut during a Friday night exodus from the city. To help facilitate the large amount of traffic during peak commuting times, Asylum's four lanes are designated as a one-way street after 4 P.M. Think super-highway inside the city limits. On this particular evening, I was stalled in the third lane out.

Horns blared as impatient drivers whipped around me, some of them shouting angry, non-repeatable phrases, as though I had deliberately planned to impede their weekend plans. Meanwhile, growing more desperate by the minute, I had managed to kill the battery by repeatedly trying to restart the engine.

I was gravely concerned that someone racing along wouldn't notice my stalled car until it was too late and plow into me, yet there was little I could do. I needed to get to a phone and call AAA, but the prospect of trying to make it safely over two lanes of rushing traffic was just too risky. Fear mounted, generating despair as I wondered where were all the police cars that normally patrolled the area.

A man in a shiny red truck pulled up alongside the passenger side and motioned for me to roll down the window.

"Stalled?"

I nodded.

"Let's give her a push," he told his buddy.

"No, please. You'll get killed," I said.

"I like to live dangerously," he joked. Slipping out of his truck, he surveyed my car, a large Lincoln which weighed about as much as a small boat.

"We're going to need some help pushing this to the side," he told his friend.

Looking around, he spied a group of sanitation workers. He let out an ear-splitting whistle. The foreman looked up. Hand motions were exchanged. The foreman nodded and shouted something to his men who turned their eyes on me. With my heart in my throat, I watched four men bravely start across the street, holding up hands to signal the traffic to stop, which to my utter amazement it did.

Within minutes, six strong men stationed themselves around my car and pushed me to safety.

The Call to Prayer

This is a fitting metaphor for the power of intercessory prayer. You have encountered a problem that is too large for you to shoulder alone. The word goes out that you are in need of help, which summons a network of prayer partners who together form a source of spiritual power that helps ferry you through your trial.

All around us are people in need of our prayers. Never a week goes by that I don't receive a prayer request. As an intercessor,

I join in their struggle. A weighty problem such as a life-threatening illness, a shaky marriage, a financial crisis, the sudden death of a loved one or any of the myriad heart-wrenching issues us mortals face are often too hard to bear alone, especially when the devil is whispering in your ear … "If there is a God, why has He allowed this to happen? Why doesn't He intervene?" Faith wavers.

In 1994, when the tragic accident took the life of our beloved three-year-old granddaughter Marissa, my faith was badly shaken. I had petitioned God each morning to protect my grandchildren and now found myself questioning why God hadn't honored that prayer.

As soon as that thought flitted through my mind, it began to grow like a virus, bringing back memories of other times when I thought God should have intervened on my behalf and didn't. My faith was shrinking as though a 1000-pound weight was compressing against my soul, yet I knew that my family was depending on my spiritual strength to get us through. Would I lose that faith during a time when those I loved needed it the most? I clung to my Rosary and called out to our Blessed Mother, who did not hesitate to call in a multitude of prayers that helped to lift me above the melee.

Later I learned that, during those first dark hours, when I stood in the midst of indescribable heartache, several of my friends were awakened in the middle of the night with the call to pray for me. Then, as the tragedy was made public, our family's name was added to prayer lists around the country.

Throughout the horrible days that followed, as I went about gathering Marissa's burial clothes, choosing a tiny white casket, walking the cemetery in search of a burial plot, I would suddenly feel a gentle rush of peace lift me above the heart-wrenching grief and I would find the strength to go on. There is absolutely no doubt in my mind that this shift of inner strength was due to the power of intercessory prayers.

We Are Encouraged to Pray for One Another

To what length would you go to intercede for a dear friend or family member?

One of my favorite Gospel stories is in Luke 5:17-26.

The place were Jesus was staying was packed with people. Pharisees had come from every village of Galilee and from Judea and Jerusalem to hear him speak.

Standing outside was a group of men, carrying a paralytic on a mat. They had heard stories of Jesus's ability to heal and decided to take their friend to him.

One could only imagine their excitement and words of encouragement as they walked through the small alleyways and along the dirt paths.

"Some say he healed a man of Leprosy," one might have said.

"I know of a man who says his brother's shriveled hand was made whole," said the other. "If he could do this, he can heal you of your paralysis. I'm certain."

But as the men neared the house where Jesus was teaching, they discovered that the crowd was so tightly packed inside that they would never get their friend through to see the Lord.

Then one of them got an inspired idea. They would climb up on the roof, remove some roof tiles and lower their friend through!

We can only imagine Jesus's reaction as he saw the paralyzed man being lowered through the roof. Perhaps it was a combination of amazement at their ingenuity coupled with delight at this great show of faith.

"I tell you, get up, take your mat and go home," Jesus says, and the Bible says that is exactly what the man did, while praising God.

Although Jesus is the sole mediator between man and God, there are many intercessors. In I Timothy 2:1-2, St. Paul urges us to continue in supplications, prayers, and intercessions for all people. In I Corinthian 3:9, he further explains that God invites us to participate in Christ's work here on earth. One way is as an intercessor on behalf of the suffering.

But why does our Father need our prayers? Surely He is more than able to handle any situation unaided.

It's similar to an earthly father who is at work in the garage fixing a lawnmower and invites his young son to help. He invites his son not because he 'needs' his son's help, but because of the fellowship linked to the task.

How Does Intercessory Prayer Differ from Other Prayers?

In intercessory prayer, we petition God's intervention on behalf of others. As I pray over a Rosary dedicated to the Ministry, I often envision the person in need as someone trying to scale a wall but not quite able to make it over. My prayers help to create a little extra 'lift.'

Exodus, Chapter 17: 8-13, provides insights into the power of intercession. While on the march out of Egypt, the Israelites were attacked by a nomadic tribe called the Amalekites. The attack was especially heinous because the Amalekites did not attack the Israelites' army, but their rear flank, which was composed mostly of women, children and the elderly.

Moses responded by instructing Joshua to march out in battle against the Amalekites. While Joshua was engaged in battle for

God's people, Moses stood on the top of a mountain with the staff of God in his hand to ensure victory. The battle raged on and Moses grew exhausted to the point that he could no longer hold up his hands; yet every time he lowered his arms, the Amalekites would begin to gain ground. As long as he held his hands aloft, Joshua and the Israelites could hold their ground.

Aaron and Hur quickly assessed the situation and interceded. They sat Moses on a rock and both men supported his hands steadily until sunset, enabling Joshua to defeat the Amalekites.

Our intercessory prayers are like that of the intercession of Aaron and Hur on behalf of Moses. They help to lift the souls of those battling against fear, disbelief, hopelessness or despair; to find new footing with renewed assurance that Jesus stands at the right hand of God and lives to make intercession for the saints here on earth.

Always Pray for One Another Without Ceasing

The Gospels are filled with stories of intercession, people seeking Jesus on behalf of others. Here is just a sampling of what has been recorded:

– A father asks Jesus to heal his epileptic son. (Matthew 17:15)
– A ruler whose daughter has just died pleads with Jesus to raise her from the dead. (Matthew 9:18)
– Simon's mother-in-law is suffering from a high fever. The disciples approach Jesus to intercede. (Luke 4:38)
– A Syrophoenician woman pleads with Jesus to heal her daughter, who is possessed by a demon. (Mark 7:26)
– At the wedding at Cana, Mary intercedes on behalf of the bridegroom when the wine is gone. (John 2)

In each recording, we note that Jesus doesn't hesitate to respond. The Father's only Son—God's representative here on earth—opens His compassionate heart to embrace the forlorn and those who suffer by healing every disease and sickness. Never once does Jesus turn anyone away.

The Power of Collective Intercessory Prayer

I have conducted this ministry for more than 20 years and can confidently say that intercessory prayer helps set into motion the necessary events, people and circumstances needed to answer the needs of those who suffer. The answer often comes by way of a 'coincidence'—a chance meeting, a book, an inspiration derived from nature that helps to lead the suffering to a new course of action or revelation.

But I've also experienced a few miracles, as intercessors have pressed on in prayer and fasting, refusing to give up—occurrences that can't be explained by fact or reason; when one knows that only God's Divine intervention could have brought this to pass. The power of unified prayer is unlimited.

One of my favorite Bible stories is found in Acts, Chapter 12. There has been a great surge of persecution of the newly formed Christians spearheaded by Herod, who has just had James put to death with a sword. When he discovers that it pleases the Jews, he has Peter arrested with the intention of bringing him to trial after the Passover. Peter is thrown into prison and shackled with chains between two soldiers. Outside his prison cell, 16 of the King's men stand guard.

Although all looks relatively hopeless, the church has gathered at John's mother's home to earnestly pray for God's intervention on

Peter's behalf. I wonder how many of those on bended knees truly believed that Peter could be saved, especially as the time for his trial drew near?

But as they were about to discover, "... *the prayer of a righteous man is powerful and effective."* (James 5:16)

The night before Peter is to stand trial, an angel appears. Peter is sleeping so soundly that the angel must strike him in the side to rouse him awake. Peter opens his eyes to a blinding light. The angel urges Peter to quickly get up. As he obeys, the chains fall from his wrists. Strangely, the two soldiers sleeping beside him are undisturbed.

"Put on your clothes and sandals," the angel instructs. "Wrap your cloak around you and follow me."

Peter assumes that he is dreaming, but does as he is told and follows the angel out of the cell. They pass two stations of guards, yet no one seems to notice their passing. It's as if they are invisible.

Finally, they come to the locked iron prison gate. Peter must think, "Well, this will end our escape for sure." But then the gates open of their own accord. Peter and the angel slip through. They walk the length of one street and the angel disappears.

The Power of Intercessory Prayer Continues Today

A CBS news report recently highlighted the power of unified prayer when it is directed toward a specific purpose.

In September of 2008, Hurricane Ike ravished Oak Island, Texas with 110-mile-per-hour winds that left mobile homes lodged among piles of trees that had been snapped like matchsticks. When it was over, 345 of the 350 homes on the Island had been destroyed, leaving victims to sleep in cars, tents, structures fashioned from the rubble and even a tugboat.

In the midst of this seemingly hopeless situation, the local pastor decided to gather the people to pray. And they came, wearing whatever they could pull from the rubble. As they stood clutching Bibles and weeping between hymns, the residents of the storm-shattered Texas coast were so intent on seeking Divine intervention that they didn't notice a stranger slip in beside them. Dressed in black, wearing a baseball cap and dark glasses, he stayed for the entire meeting before quietly slipping away. That stranger was the singer Neil Diamond.

Diamond was scheduled to give a concert in nearby Houston and, on a whim, decided to take a drive to the Gulf to witness firsthand the devastation that had been caused by Ike. As he walked among the ruins, he came upon the prayer meeting. Greatly moved with compassion, Diamond decided to pledge the sales of his concert merchandise to help rebuild. The sales raised $1.7 million, enough to restore several of the homes that had been destroyed by the storm.

As I ponder this story, I'm struck immediately by the series of events that took place in order to bring about Diamond's offer of assistance. First, the famous singer had a concert booked near enough that he was able to visit the site. He would also have to have been sufficiently curious about the devastation that had taken place to take the time out of his busy schedule to drive the distance from Houston all the way to the Texas shoreline to check it out.

The preacher was moved to conduct a prayer meeting, asking for God's intervention. Diamond just 'happened' to be there at the particular time to hear the plea— and that moved him with compassion. He also had to be a person with access to the necessary funds needed to meet the people's prayers to rebuild.

At any one of these junctures—had Diamond not accepted the concert date in Houston, or canceled, or the Hurricane hit after his concert, or there had been a traffic jam that kept him from the prayer service or any number of myriad events—the outcome could have been changed.

As I said …

When we join together in intercessory prayer, miracles often do happen. ॐ

Chapter 8

The Ministry of the Holy Rosary Is ...

*– The most powerful and unique form
of intercessory prayer*

ॐ

On August 6, 1945 at 8:15am, a B-29 bomber dropped the first atomic bomb on Hiroshima. A half mile away from the epicenter, eight Jesuit priests stationed at Our Lady's Assumption Church were in various modes of preparing for what they assumed would be a normal day when they noticed a bright flash of light. One priest later explained that he thought an explosion had taken place at the harbor, which was a chief supply port to Japanese submarines.

Seconds later, a sudden, earth-shattering explosion sent the priests hurtling through the air. One man likened it to a leaf being turned round and round in a gust of autumn wind. When it was over, the men rushed outside to a scene of unimaginable devastation. Two thirds of the city had been destroyed, and an estimated 110,000 victims instantly incinerated. Miraculously, Our Lady of Assumption Church and the eight priests were unharmed.

A band of US Army Medical experts later examined the priests and was at a loss to explain how these men had escaped the signs normally associated with exposure to elevated radiation levels. Over the next 30 years, scientists continued to monitor the priests, performing more than 200 exams; none of the priests ever suffered from the cancers so prevalent among survivors.

How can this be explained?

Father Hubert Shiffer, one of the eight priests who survived unscathed, attributed it to their devotion to the Blessed Mother through the Rosary. He felt that Mary had surrounded them with a protective shield that had made them impervious to the blast and the radiation poisoning that followed.*

If that is so, what made the prayers of the Rosary so effective that it could circumvent the physical effects of being exposed to an atomic blast?

Why Is the Rosary Such a Powerful Intercessory Prayer?

When I began the Ministry of the Holy Rosary, I was immediately struck by the coincidental meetings that aligned me with those in need of encouragement and hope. Later, I would be filled with the same kind of awe as stories filtered back showing how the Rosary had impacted these people's lives and met their most heartfelt needs. Further intriguing were the times that I felt led to pray for healing, renewal, peace, or reconciliation only to discover later that, when Mary's intended recipients arrived, they had been in need of just that particular grace.

The more Rosaries I prayed over and presented, the more questions I had.

For instance, how did people just happen across my path when they were in need?

Three days later, the US dropped a larger atomic bomb on Nagasaki. 74,000 people were instantly killed; yet it is interesting to note that a Franciscan Friary established by St. Maximilian Kolbe was unharmed and that its occupants suffered no ill effects. The Brothers attributed this miracle to their devotion to the Rosary.

Why was the reaction to the gift always the same? Tears. Looks of disbelief as they realized that God was ever-present in their suffering.

And what about the stories? Those of peace, revelation and healing that seemed to follow this gift?

There could be only one conclusion. Something extraordinary happened when I interceded through the Rosary on behalf of the suffering—something that didn't happen when I simply lifted up a person in prayer. But what was it?

The Power of a Mother's Petitions

Whenever I pray the Luminous Mysteries and come to the Wedding of Cana, I picture Mary in my mind's eye, enjoying the company of family and friends who are gathered to join in the celebration of a newly married couple about to embark on their own journey. I wonder if her thoughts hasten back to her own wedding day, when there had been so many unanswered questions. She and Joseph must have wondered, why had God set them to parent the Messiah? Would they be adequate to the task?

Perhaps she glances at her Son at this wedding. He smiles her way and she experiences that special bond between a mother and child. For nine months, she had carried him in her womb, a Holy Tabernacle not made of mortar or stone yet made by the hands of God. Immaculate Mary conceived without sin.

Love floods her heart. How very proud she is of Jesus, yet also fearful. She tries not to think about what must come or the words of Simeon on the day of Jesus's presentation at the temple ...

"... this child is destined to cause the falling and rising of many in Israel, and to be a sign that will be spoken against, so that the

thoughts of many hearts will be revealed. And a sword will pierce your own soul too."

Luke 2:34-35

She knows that the sands of time have quickly passed since that day, and that all too soon Jesus must begin his ministry. It will be a dangerous ministry, with so much political unrest, yet she reminds herself that it is for this very reason He has come.

Then a servant bends to whisper in her ear. "The wine is running out."

She glances across the courtyard. The young bridegroom is engaged in a lively conversation with his new father-in-law. How embarrassed he will be when his guests discover that the wine jugs are empty, she thinks.

Mary brushes aside her veil, leans across the table and gently taps her Son's arm. He had been conversing with his disciples. Seeing her concern, he asks, "What is it, Mother?"

She nods toward the servant holding an empty pitcher. "The wine has run out."

I can picture Jesus's gentle smile as He gazes at the familiar, beloved face. Perhaps He runs a tender hand along her cheek as He asks softly, teasingly, "Woman, how does your concern affect me? My hour has not yet come."

Perhaps not, but she knows that it is drawing near. Hasn't she always known? God has not asked her to shelter Him from the very role that He has come to play, but to ready Him, and she has been faithful by living out the tenets of her deeply rooted faith through her Mother's heart. It is the same, tender heart that now floods with compassion for the bridegroom, wishing to save him embarrassment.

She beckons to a servant. "Do whatever he tells you."

The servant hurries over and waits. Jesus smiles and shakes his head with affection. Although it is not His time, Jesus cannot deny His beloved Mother. His love for her transcends all barriers.

"Bring those barrels of water over here," He tells the servant. And His ministry begins.

Mary's Place with Her Son

At first, the story of wine running out at a wedding appears so trivial that the reader must wonder why John thought it necessary to include in his Gospel. Unlike all the other accounts of Jesus's ministry, this had nothing to do with the revelation of the Father's love, or living a truly righteous life, or how to enter into the gift of salvation.

True, should the wine run out, the bridegroom would suffer embarrassment, but this is hardly a desperate situation. Life will go on—which might be why Jesus points out that the time of miracles proclaiming His Divinity has not yet arrived.

Then why, instead, does He decide to advance God's timetable at the request of His Mother?

Since the Bible is 'spirit breathed' and inspired by God, written for: *"... teaching, rebuking, correcting and training in righteousness so that the man of God may be thoroughly equipped for every good work."* (2 Timothy 3:16), let us ask ourselves, then, what is the message that God wishes to convey?

Was not the inclusion of the story of the Wedding of Cana designed to showcase Mary's powerfully intercessory role in the redemption of mankind? Through her compassionate heart, she asks Jesus to intercede. And her Son complies even though it means launching His ministry prematurely. Once the miracle is performed, the countdown to Calvary begins.

Through Mary's intercession, the gift of salvation is that much closer, even though it will mean the loss of her precious Son on the Cross that much sooner. What mother who is told that her child is about to die wouldn't wish to prolong his time here on earth, even if it meant for just a day or even an hour?

Mary's request is really her great sacrifice, a living example that summarizes the core of Jesus's message of a Father's love. Like the Father who would not deny the sacrifice of His only son so others might live, Mary does not withhold the precious days and hours she might still have if it means bringing deliverance to God's family that much sooner.

Mary lived during one of the most tumultuous times in her people's history. Her suffering heart had witnessed neighbors sold into slavery and families thrown out of their homes, their land confiscated when they were unable to pay the heavy taxes placed on them by Herod. And above the holocaust, fervent prayers rose like incense for the deliverance by their long-awaited Messiah.

The same love shared by the Father for His people, which caused Mary to risk all to say yes to God's call, propels her now to hasten the advent of her Son's destiny. It is this—the greatest sacrifice a mother's heart can be called upon to render—that has earned her the right to be called "Blessed." And it is why Jesus cannot deny her any request. Her love for God's people has only grown since that wedding feast. It is her desire to see all saved and none perish, to ameliorate man's pain and suffering. Mary's Rosary is an astonishingly powerful devotional prayer because of the salvation made possible through the sacrifice of her beloved Son. ᗱ

Chapter 9

The Ministry of the Holy Rosary Is ...

– *The Collective Power of Prayer*

ॐ

On July 2, 2009, newscaster Bob Barnard of Fox 5 News reported that the Archdiocese of Baltimore was preparing to request a Vatican investigation involving a modern-day miracle that was being attributed to Blessed Francis Xavier Seelos. It was through his intercession that Mary Ellen Heibel contends that she was cured from terminal cancer.

Five years ago, Heibel was told by doctors that there was no hope of survival from the cancer that had metastasized throughout her entire body.

"It had spread to my liver, two places in one lung and the other lung," she said. "My back and my sternum, too."

Then a friend suggested that she pray to Francis Seelos, the 19th century priest who had worked at her parish, St. Mary's, during the 1860's. His image adorns one of the church's fine stained-glass windows. Blessed Francis Seelos was beatified by Pope John Paul II in 2000.

Within a week of Heibel's soliciting his intercession, a CAT scan revealed that all the tumors had disappeared. Since then, Heibel has remained cancer free.

Spontaneous remission? Coincidence? Medical anomaly? Or was the cure the result of seeking the intercession of the saint?

Intercession of the Saints by Jesus's Example

Luke 9:28-36 records the Transfiguration. Peter, James, and John have accompanied Jesus up to a mountain to pray. Tired, they fall asleep, but later awaken to see Jesus bathed in a bright flash of light and conversing with two men, whom they recognize as Moses and Elijah. As the disciples look on transfixed, these men begin to converse with Jesus about His upcoming death in Jerusalem and the fulfillment of His earthly mission. During the end of this encounter, the disciples hear the voice of God coming from a cloud as He proclaims that Jesus is His Son and that they were to ... *"listen to him."*

But another, more subtle message is being conveyed in this tableau. Through this heavenly encounter with two of the Old Testament's most powerful prophets, Jesus reveals the availability of the saints to act on our behalf.

In Hebrews 12:1, St. Paul supports this message when he writes that the saints are still in contact with what's happening here on earth:

"Therefore, since we are surrounded by such a great cloud of witnesses, let us throw off everything that hinders and the sin that so easily entangles, and let us run with perseverance the race marked out for us ..."

One translation of this message states that they are *"cheering us on."* I like that image. The saints, who had dedicated their lives to promoting God's great plan of redemption through Jesus Christ while on earth, continue this work in heaven through the power of their intercessory prayers.

What makes their prayers so powerful?

James 5:16 provides insight when he writes, *"... the prayer of a righteous man is powerful and effective."*

This scripture highlights the special audience God gives to the prayers of the saints—those men and women who have given their all for the Gospel or who have lived exemplary lives through their service.

When Jesus gave Mary into John's care at the foot of the cross, He secured Mary's place of honor among the saints. Collectively this Communion of Saints stands always at the ready to hearken to her requests when she is asked by petitioners to intercede on their behalf.

Intercession of the Celestial Court

Known as the Queen of Angels, Mary revealed to the children at Fatima that advocates of the Rosary would be given special access through her requests to the entire Celestial Court. These heavenly angelic beings, who possess a wide range of gifts, make their powers available to Mary.

The first time I understood the power of this grace was when Helena, one of my readers, wrote to share an interesting story. Her mother-in-law, whom we'll call Emily, was in the hospital; she was in her late eighties and dying. She was a faithful Catholic and was not afraid of death; however, she was greatly disturbed that her last days might be spent within the cold, sterile walls of a nursing home. As she told her daughter-in-law, "If I have to die, I want it to be in my own bed."

Unfortunately, Emily's condition was so serious and her medical needs so great that her wish to die at home in her own bed could not be granted. And so it was that, with a heavy heart, the family gathered one evening in her hospital room to break the news that she was being transferred the next morning to a nursing home.

Although those at her bedside pledged to visit every day, Emily couldn't contain her grief.

"God has abandoned me," she lamented, tears streaming down her wrinkled cheeks.

Helena went on to say that the scene was heart-wrenching.

"Dying at home, surrounded by her personal effects and familiar surroundings was the one thing Emily had requested; yet it was the one thing that we could not in good conscience provide."

That night when visiting hours were over, family members left with sad hearts and a promise that they would return in the morning to escort her to her new home.

"As promised, we all gathered in the hospital waiting room the next morning," Helena wrote. "I don't think any of us got any sleep that night. We looked like death warmed over."

Finally, they could delay the moment no longer and began the short trek down the hospital corridors toward Emily's room, each personally dreading what they would find.

Soberly, they filed into Emily's room, expecting to find a woman filled with fear. Much to their surprise, however, they found her seated up in bed, brightly smiling as the nurse went about the process of readying her for transport.

"Come in," she called, waving them in. "Isn't this a wonderful morning for a ride?"

Helena said her first thought was…"I don't know what kind of meds they've given her, but I hope they last."

The nurse told the group that the ambulance transport would be arriving in a few minutes, then noting their quizzical faces, she said,

"Emily, why don't you tell your family about the visitor you had last night."

Then, with a smile, the nurse left.

"Oh, yes ... my visitor," the elderly woman began, glancing up at the ceiling with a faraway look in her eyes as though replaying the scene frame by frame.

"I was having a hard time getting to sleep last night. You all know how I feel about nursing homes. I didn't want to die in a strange place," she began.

Her family members solemnly nodded, their faces reflecting the deep sorrow associated with this decision.

"I tossed and turned for hours. Even the sleeping pill they gave me didn't seem to help. Then, around one o'clock, the door slowly swung open and a young gentleman came in rolling a book cart. He knew my name and said he'd heard that I was having trouble getting to sleep. I just assumed that he had spoken with the nurses. There's one in particular that had been especially kind.

"Anyway, he asked if I would like some company. I said I'd welcome a visit, so he sat right here," she patted the bed, her eyes softening with the memory.

"There was something so peaceful about his presence that I found myself telling him all about my fears. We sat and talked for quite a while. Finally, he got up and walked over to the book cart. He said that he had something that would help me feel better. When he handed me a book, I reminded him that I was leaving tomorrow and would have no way of returning it. But he insisted and said it was for me to keep.

"I stayed up the rest of the night reading this book." The soft covered book had been lying beside her. She handed it to her son. "It was just like he said. As soon as I started reading it, I felt at peace."

While the others pressed Emily for more details, Helena headed out to the nurse's station to find the young man's name and address. At the very least, she felt he deserved a thank-you note.

The same nurse who had been attending Emily was seated at the front desk. She saw Helena coming and smiled.

"You want to know the name of Emily's visitor," she said without preamble and with a twinkle in her eye.

"I can't believe the change. We were all dreading today. I must thank him properly." Helena explained.

The nurse's smile broadened. "There's just one problem."

"Problem?"

"There was no visitor last night."

"But she said ..."

"I asked the head night nurse. She swears no one went in or out of your mother-in-law's room. I've known this co-worker for 20 years. Nothing gets past her, especially visitors on the floor after visiting hours."

"But the book ..."

"That's another mystery. We don't have a book cart and we certainly wouldn't have allowed a volunteer into a patient's room that late at night even if we had."

"I saw the book.* Someone must have given it to her. How do you explain it?"

The nurse paused a moment, then leaned forward and whispered, "Do you believe in angels?"

Emily went to be with the Lord a few weeks later. The nursing-home staff said that, even though her stay was short, she had brought the gift of faith and hope to all those who attended her.

---

* *The book was one I had written, entitled "Grace Will Lead Me Home."*

Did Mary send an angel through the intercessory prayers of both her family and the Rosaries being said on Emily's behalf to help vanquish her fears and great sorrow at not being allowed to go home to die? St. Augustine stated that the Archangel St. Michael stands ready to do battle with the forces of evil on Mary's behalf.

But why is this connection with the Celestial Court such an integral part of the Ministry of the Holy Rosary?

St. Paul in Ephesians 6:12 provides insight into the ongoing spiritual battles for our souls and the erosion of our faith that takes place behind the scenes:

"For our struggle is not against flesh and blood, but against the rulers, against the authorities, against the powers of this dark world and against the spiritual forces of evil in the heavenly realms."

But how do these battles affect the efficacy of our intercessory prayers?

Daniel 10:12-14 provides a glimpse into this warfare and how it can keep our prayers from being answered. In this passage, an angel is sent to give a message to Daniel:

"Do not be afraid, Daniel. Since the first day that you set your mind to gain understanding and to humble yourself before your God, your words were heard and I have come in response to them. But the prince of the Persian kingdom (Satan) resisted me twenty-one days. Then Michael (the Archangel), one of the chief princes, came to help me because I was detained there with the king of Persia."

I remember a personal incident that shows the power of Mary's Rosary to combat the powers of evil. I've shared with you the tragic accident in which our granddaughter Marissa was killed when she ran behind a truck our son was backing up. Upon hearing the devastating news, I asked my husband to drive while I prayed the Rosary. Later I discovered that, at that exact time that I was praying, our son had locked himself in a room with a shotgun, ready to commit suicide. It is my belief that Mary called upon St. Michael to intervene and push back the powers of darkness, which saved our son.

Mary's Queenship of the Angels allows her to act as a shield to defend the efficacy of our intercessory prayers. In this role, Mary, ever vigilant, sends help to those who are discouraged or who question God's infinite love. And, perhaps, that help sometimes arrives by way of a special stranger bearing the gift of peace and wheeling a cart of books.

Empowered by the Holy Spirit

"Do not leave Jerusalem, but wait for the gift my Father promised, which you have heard me speak about. For John baptized with water, but in a few days you will be baptized with the Holy Spirit." Acts 1: 4-5

"... you will receive power when the Holy Spirit comes on you; and you will be my witnesses ..." Acts 1:8

On the day of Pentecost, the Holy Spirit came bearing wonderful and varied gifts that would empower followers for service. The Book of Acts chronicles the importance of His role and those gifts.

In Acts 8: 26-40, the Holy Spirit prompts Philip to go south along a desert road where he meets an Ethiopian eunuch trying to decipher the meaning behind a passage taken from Isaiah that foretold Jesus's death. *"The Spirit told Philip, 'Go to that chariot and stay near.'"* Philip obeys and is given the opportunity to explain the fulfillment of the passage through Jesus. The man is converted.

The Holy Spirit's role is of great importance to the Ministry of the Holy Rosary. From the beginning, He has bestowed gifts that have allowed me to effectively minister to those who are sent across my path

I often marvel at the 'coincidences' that have placed me at a particular location where I encounter a person in need of God's comfort. I've shared with you the time my daughter and I just 'happened' to be in the baby aisle at Wal-Mart's, met the woman in need of advice in choosing a gift and listened to her tell about the young mother who was going through a horrendous trial, which prompted me to offer a Rosary.

Jesus said that the Holy Spirit would also teach us to pray. (Luke 12:12). He gave me words to say to the unbelieving Morty that deeply resonated within his soul and provided comfort during a fearful time. And the Holy Spirit has often led me to pray my Rosary for a specific grace such as healing, or reconciliation or simply peace. Later, when I hand off that particular Rosary, I am always amazed to discover it was just that grace that was needed the most.

I remember an incident when I had been called to pray for peace with my Rosary. I then met a young woman whose husband had just died, leaving her a widow with four small children, one of whom suffered from autism. Although this woman had a plethora of needs, after a short conversation it was quite evident that what was essential to calming her troubled soul was the good Lord's peace.

Those who work promoting the Ministry of the Holy Rosary have been empowered by the Holy Spirit with a wide range of gifts we can give to those who are suffering—and rightly so, since the Holy Spirit is also Mary's beloved Spouse. ॐ

Chapter 10

The Ministry of the Holy Rosary Is ...

– *Personal Transforming Power*

ॐ

W hat began as a simple intercessory prayer ministry several decades ago has expanded in ways that amaze me. Like a pebble tossed in a pond, this ministry had rippled out, transforming hundreds and hundreds of lives, and flooding my heart with an unspeakable joy.

No longer do the recipients of these Rosaries simply 'hope' that God hears and answers prayers. They know He does, having personally been touched by God's physical response to their pain through Mary's beloved devotional.

But the recipients aren't the only ones whose lives have been transformed. When I look back over the years or read the prayer journals that log my ongoing journey, I am struck by the enormous impact this ministry has had on my spiritual life.

Those Who Are Called Are Refashioned

The Bible is rich with stories of those called out to serve God in ministry and of the refining process that followed.

In Genesis, Joseph the son of Jacob begins as something of a brash young braggart. As the favored son, he struts around in a specially made coat of many colors and can't wait to tell his brothers of a heavenly vision that foretells how one day they will be made to bow down to him.

Although the prophecy is true, Joseph will not rule as a sovereign, but as God's servant who is refined by a series of harsh injustices. Through these events, Joseph is imbued with the graces needed to better serve God's people.

In Exodus we meet Moses, who is called by God to lead the Israelites out of bondage. He, too, will be transformed along the way: from a quick-tempered zealot who would take matters into his own hand, to a long-suffering leader.

Those who choose to offer themselves as ministers of the Ministry of the Holy Rosary can also expect to be transformed. Now, I don't mean to imply that they will be thrown into prison or made to spend 40 years wandering in the desert. But those who wish to be ambassadors of God's grace through this special Marian devotional must be open to God's refinement.

As a deeply spiritual woman once said, "God doesn't need silver vessels to fill for His service. He needs *yielded* vessels, those individuals who are willing to remove any impediment that might separate them from the fullness of His grace no matter how difficult the task."

Moments of Personal Transformation

Mary speaks most directly to my heart while I am praying the Rosary. Down through the years, She has made me aware of several areas that needed a tweaking. For instance, my tendency to assess others by externals—the way they speak, or their social graces or, in some cases, lack of them. Then there's the issue of my impatience with anything or anyone who doesn't move with the speed of light. I grew up in New York.

There is one issue, however, that Mary pointed out a decade ago that speaks to the profound personal transforming power of this ministry. Although it was the hardest task I was ever assigned, when it was resolved, it led me to a deeper, more profound connection with the Lord. Looking back, I'm glad that I persevered.

One Sunday morning after Mass, a choir member asked if I would pray for her mother. She had just been diagnosed with thyroid cancer. Since I had nearly lost my life to thyroid cancer, she knew that I would take the request to heart.

Monday morning found me seated in my favorite chair with Rosary in hand as I remembered my own encounter with this dreaded disease. Suddenly, all the emotions associated with that battle came flooding back. It made me more determined than ever to storm heaven's gates on behalf of this woman.

I prayed one decade, then another and was just about to begin the third, when I heard Mary's voice most clearly speak to my heart.

You must find forgiveness for your mother before my Son can respond to your prayers.

My mother??? What did my relationship with my mother have to do with the intercessor prayers that I was offering up for this woman?

"I don't understand," I told Mary.

Until you can forgive your mother from your heart your gift of prayers cannot appropriate the intercession you seek.

As I pondered this, the Holy Spirit reminded me of the words Jesus had spoken about forgiveness.

"Therefore, if you are offering your gift at the altar and there remember that your brother has something against you, leave your gift there in front of the altar. First go and be reconciled with your brother; then come and offer your gift."

Matthew 5:23-24

I placed the Rosary aside and felt the old resentments that stir whenever my mother is mentioned. I had always been obedient to Mary's promptings, but this time I feared that I might fail her.

My mother and I had had a tumultuous past. Both my parents were alcoholics, although they would have been shocked to hear me say that, since they believed that if they functioned during the day, they were merely social drinkers. True, my father managed to get up every morning and make it to work. He was a carpenter. And my mother kept an immaculate house and made sure we girls were always spotlessly dressed. It was just the nights and weekends that were filled with drunken rages.

As horrible as that was to endure as a child, harder still was the complete absence of my mother's love. It wasn't that she was incapable of loving. She lavished praise and attention on my three sisters. It was just me whom she denied.

In 1990, my mother developed liver cancer and knew she was dying. She gathered my sisters together and told them the news, then made them swear that they would not tell me until after she had passed on. To the very end, I was denied her affection.

The pain of that decision haunted me for years. I would have given anything to have been able to say goodbye. But even more heartbreaking was the coded message in my mother's final decision that I simply did not matter. Over the years, that hurt continued to bleed like an open wound. So when Mary told me that my prayers would not be heard until I found a way to forgive my mother with my 'heart,' I felt it would have been easier if she had asked me to walk on a bed of nails.

It wasn't that I didn't want to forgive my mother. In fact, I forgave her daily. But I could never get to the place where, when I thought of her, I wasn't filled with a deep-seated anger. As the mother of three children, I couldn't imagine treating one of them with such complete disregard for how my actions would color their lives.

It took me several weeks before I could begin the journey to find the forgiveness that Jesus demanded of me. In the beginning, I spent a great deal of time searching for an escape clause, anything but deal with the deep inner pain.

First I reminded God that I had tried to forgive her. Wasn't 'trying' enough? Next, I insisted that I didn't really feel unforgiveness in my heart for my mother. I was just deeply hurt. There was a difference, right?

But in the end, my love of the Lord and my passion to serve Him overcame my need to circumvent the issue. I had given my life to Him without reservation and He had accepted, which meant that He was now free to refashion my soul in the image of His beloved son.

I did not know why my mother found it impossible to love me, that she would bar me from her deathbed and not feel the need to say goodbye. But that was not the issue. The issue was could I forgive her for what she had done? Jesus's words uttered from the cross became my lodestone …

"Forgive them Father for they know not what they do."

Mary led me to the Sacrament of Reconciliation and, through a heartfelt confession of my anger, unforgiveness and yes … even hatred … I finally found the release I sought. Through the grace received by absolution, I began to focus my attention on my mother as the spirit God had breathed life into, who had been filled with endless possibilities and who was not the woman that she had allowed herself to become.

This is the image I now keep in my mind as I pray for her soul. That of a spirit so greatly loved by the Father that, if she had been the only soul in jeopardy of ever perishing, He would have *still* sent His beloved Son to die on the Cross just for her. How can I forgive any less?

With this resolution, I was finally able to pray for the choir member's poor mother and filled a Rosary with prayers for healing, which our dear Lord honored. She recently died and her daughter told me that they buried her with the Rosary that Mary had sent her way.

Keeping the Sabbath Holy and Other Lessons I Learned

One day, while reading through Exodus, I came upon the Ten Commandments and read God's decree about keeping the Sabbath.

"Remember the Sabbath Day by keeping it holy. Six days you shall labor and do all your work, but the seventh day is a Sabbath to the Lord, your God. On it you shall not do any work, neither you nor your son, or daughter, nor your manservant or maidservant, nor your animals, nor the alien within your gates. For in six days the Lord made the heavens and the earth, the sea and all that is in them; but He rested on the seventh day. Therefore the Lord blessed the Sabbath and made it holy."

Exodus 20:8

Before American society became consumer obsessed, Sundays were spent visiting with family. Most of it centered around the dinner table. Sunday mornings before church, a pot roast or chicken was set in the oven on low (this was before crockpots and microwaves). The dining-room table would be set with the best linen and china. Grandma's silver would have been polished to a high gloss and carefully placed alongside each plate.

After church, children would hurriedly change into their play clothes, then wait on the front porch for the cousins to arrive along with grandparents and aunts and uncles who came bearing sinfully delicious cakes, baskets of warm yeast rolls and quarts of fresh produce straight from the family garden.

While the women gathered in the kitchen to put the finishing touches to dinner, the men would loosen their ties and sit around the living room or, if the weather permitted, on the front porch to talk about the week's political events. Occasionally, a husband would call to his wife and complain that they were about to faint from hunger.

Dinner time was a lively affair. Platters heaped high with family favorites were consumed with gusto. But, aside from the food, it was the conversation most people relished. Someone might begin with the weekly news from their household, someone else would talk about their job, or the weather, and conversation would eventually segue into stories about the family's heritage.

Many homes along Chester Street, where I grew up, were owned by second-generation immigrants. I was often privileged to be included during these Sunday gatherings among our neighbors. I loved to sit quietly and listen to the elders share their firsthand accounts of life in the 'old' country and to talk with a spirit of gratefulness at having found refuge in America. As three and sometimes four generations listened and shared, these stories affirmed their connectedness.

Today, these Sunday get-togethers are a thing of the past, mostly reserved for holidays or birthdays. Families nowadays spend the Sabbath catching up on chores, shopping at the malls or going to soccer practice. Somehow these do not seem to fit the command to "keep the Sabbath holy." So what does?

For me, it does not mean spending the entire day in prayer or some other strict observance. Even Jesus was more interested in the heart of the law than in the law itself. I do find, however, that if I begin each Sunday morning by asking myself how I plan to spend my day, it helps to keep me more God-centered.

For instance, I enjoy spending time with those I love on Sunday. My husband Paul and I might plan a picnic lunch, or take the dogs for a walk, or cuddle on the sofa. I also try to have my family over for Sunday dinners at least once a month. Most are casual affairs. I no longer go all out with rib roasts and fancy desserts. And in the summer, we do a lot of barbecuing.

Occasionally, while we're all gathered around the table, I'll take out an old photo album and Paul will share stories of his family, who had arrived on the shores of Long Island in 1698.

As with so many of Mary's promptings, keeping the Sabbath holy is an ongoing process of spiritual refinement. I'm still trying. Just being aware of the commandment to keep the day holy makes me look at my choices more carefully. I no longer eat out on Sundays or do anything that would cause another person to have to abandon keeping the holy day. (Oh … all right … maybe on Easter and Mother's Day. And there is that occasional rainy-day movie. Remember, I'm still a work in progress.)

I do try never to shop on Sundays and don't miss it a bit except when our area garden centers are open. I'm an avid gardener.

Through the years, Mary has also made me acutely aware of how I present myself to the world. I find myself questioning purchases that I might never have questioned before.

I'm not a shopaholic, but I do like fine, classic clothing. There's nothing wrong with that. But I have discovered that while an Ann Taylor suit might be just the ticket to impress a possible donor to the local community theater, that upscale suit can be a real turn-off if I'm trying to encourage a couple who are down on their luck to trust God to provide.

This has also lead me to question other areas—the type of car I drive. The house I live in. God has no issue with living well. After all, He created this world and all that is in it for our benefit and enjoyment. But when we purchase items to separate ourselves from others or elevate us in a way that says 'we're special' or 'better,' we are outside of God's grace and no longer can be effective in Mary's service.

The Rewards for Giving Your All

It may appear to some that being a minister for Mary is difficult, and at times it is—but the rewards are far greater. Although the process is ongoing and will take a lifetime, there can be no greater joy. Whenever I place a Rosary into the hands of one who suffers and look into his or her eyes to see hope rekindled, my heart floods with praise. At that moment, I feel Mary's hand upon my life, refashioning it for service so that, by God's grace, I may become a vessel through which others might be blessed. ॐ

Chapter 11

The Ministry of the Holy Rosary Is …

– *When you are called to join in*

❧

Perhaps, as you've read the stories of those who have been forever impacted by the Ministry of the Holy Rosary, you've felt a tug on your heart, an inner longing to offer yourself for Mary's service. But you feel hesitant. How do you know if you're truly called to the ministry? After all, you've never felt any special power when you've interceded for others in the past.

And what if you *do* offer your services? You're uncertain if you could find the courage to go up to a complete stranger and offer a token of your Catholic faith? Catholics are the quiet Christians, remember? They're not comfortable sharing their faith with others. As I have said, I had the same misgivings the first time I offered a Rosary. To my rational mind, it seemed a silly thing to do. I was seated in a Protestant church, not a Catholic Cathedral. Everyone would be watching. What if the homeless woman turned me away? Besides, how did I know that the inner voice I had heard was Mary's and not mine? Then there was the scary prospect of actually having to walk across the aisle to offer her the Rosary.

Come as Little Children

Jesus said, *"Unless you come to me as little children...."*

Children bring a wide-eyed wonderment to life and are totally uninhibited when it comes to trying new things. I find it interesting that Mary has often given children messages to share with the world, such as at Fatima and Lourdes. Is it the child-like openness that she seeks?

These child visionaries were not expected to understand why they were chosen or to know how they were to accomplish what she employed them to do. They simply said 'yes' to her call, then trusted Mary to work out the details. And so it is with those who accept her call to the Ministry of the Holy Rosary.

The only caution I might add when you are accepting the call is this: Do so with great humility and avoid all temptation to feel special or divinely empowered above others. Like Mary, ministers should be content to stand in the background. We are but bearers of Jesus's light, commissioned to extend the Father's message of eternal love and infinite compassion for those who suffer.

How do I know that I've been truly called?

Remember, the Bible says that ... *"all have been called."* God has called all of us to help further the message of salvation to a suffering world.

What kind of a commitment must I make?

The commitment is entirely up to you, the lay minister. Some called to the ministry may wish to commit for just a specific period of time, such as Advent or Lent, while others may carry it forward as an ongoing ministry.

How do I begin?

It's always best to begin with quiet reflection and prayer. Some may wish to make a small retreat, or set aside a day spent in solitude with prayer and fasting.

During this time, you might search any misgivings or concerns. For instance, ask yourself if you are willing to override any hesitancy you might have in sharing your faith when called to offer a Rosary. In the beginning, I had myriad fears and reservations but, once I made the decision to do it, the rewards were so great that all the misgivings quickly dissolved.

Finally, those who feel called to the ministry must be willing to set aside a specific time every day to pray the Rosary. This is paramount if you wish to be an effective minister of the Ministry of the Holy Rosary. Prayers should not be hurried. Each should be a heart-felt petition on behalf of the recipient.

A word of warning about this...

Satan is at war against God's people and knows the power behind the Rosary. He will do everything in his power to keep you from this dedicated time of prayer.

In the beginning when I would pray the Rosary, the dogs would suddenly declare an emergency and need to go out. The phone would ring (even though I could swear that it had been turned off). The caller usually had an urgent request that I 'drop everything' and tend to a certain issue. Once, I turned on the self-cleaning function of my oven just before prayer time and within seconds the house was enveloped in a black coat of smoke.

Now when I begin my intercessory prayer time, I make certain that the dogs are walked beforehand; hubby knows where to find the car keys, and I refrain from all forms of multi-tasking including cleaning the oven. Even then, there are times when I'm interrupted. On those occasions, I attend to whatever needs attending to, then begin again where I left off.

Be persistent. No matter how many times you may be interrupted, continue until you have finished the five mysteries for that day.

What kind of Rosary should I choose?

Since this Rosary is an extension of Mary's intercession for a much-loved soul, it should be chosen with care. Set aside a specific time to shop. Make it a celebratory experience. This is not just a strand of ordinary beads but will become a Holy Vessel; a physical sign of a Mother's boundless love and a faith in her Son's power to answer every need. It should be special.

I always ask the salespeople to allow me to hold the strand before making a final decision. Strange as this might seem, the Rosary needs to 'feel right.'

That doesn't mean that this Rosary should be expensive. I've purchased ten-dollar pewter-like strands with a nicely shaped crucifix, and Italian glass beads for thirty. I've also purchased beautiful 'used' strands at tag sales for a dollar. In the end, the choice is entirely up to you.

Does this chosen Rosary need to be blessed by a priest?

Religious articles, including the Rosary when blessed, are set apart from the ordinary. The blessing bestowed by the Church will make this Rosary a sacramental. Using a sacramental confers help from God to grow in holiness, which is especially beneficial to the souls for whom you are interceding.

How will I know when I've prayed enough over this Rosary?

Prayers are such a personal thing that I find it difficult to advise how long you should pray, or to give you an exact 'formula' for praying over a Rosary. From the beginning, I have simply prayed over the beads until I felt as though I needn't pray any longer. I know this is kind of a doughy response to an earnest question, which is why I sought Mary's advice when urged to take this powerful devotional public. In response, she gave me the Novena of the Holy Rosary for those who wish a more structured system of prayer. You will find it on my webpage at: www.katherine valentine.com.

In the beginning, you might begin with the Novena. Then at other times you might switch to praying until you feel as though no additional prayers are needed. Or you might switch back and forth between the two methods of prayer. Either way is fine.

I usually pray over a Rosary for a month or more before I feel that no additional prayers are needed. But again, there is no right or wrong. Just trust Mary to lead.

How long does it take before Mary sends along the recipient?

I have held onto a Rosary for months before I felt the familiar *push*. At other times I have just finished the prayers, stepped out my front door—and Mary sent the recipient along.

How will I recognize the recipient?

Mary will guide you. For instance …

You'll be standing in a supermarket line and someone will begin to share a problem they've been facing. Your heart fills with compassion and you feel a gentle mental nudge to offer the Rosary.

Or, you feel drawn to a person seated on a park bench. Polite conversation begins. Without prompting, this person shares his or her feelings of despair. You remember the Rosary that's inside your pocket and feel compelled to offer it for comfort.

This is just a sampling. The scenarios differ widely.

But one thing I have noticed. Whenever the recipient arrives, everyone else disappears. For instance, you'll be in a crowded department store with clusters of people all around; yet when the recipient appears, the crowds move off to one side.

What do I say as I offer the Rosary?

I usually repeat the same words that were given to me that first day.

"This is filled with prayers. I hope they give you comfort."

But you should feel free to use whatever phrase seems most natural to you. Don't forget, the Holy Spirit's presence is deeply imbedded in this ministry. We have His promise that, when words fail us, He will teach us what to say.

What if they refuse the Rosary?

In all the years that I've worked for Mary through this ministry, only once did someone refuse the gift. To that person I simply replied, "I'm sorry for your pain and will continue to pray for you," then walked away.

If you offer this precious gift and it is refused, don't let it shake your faith in the ministry or your ability to interpret Mary's promptings. In my case, I saw a person whom Mary greatly loved and had sent my way with an offering of prayer but who chose to reject the gift. Afterward, I prayed that this offer (although refused) would serve as a reminder of God's ever-present love. One never knows what kind of impact, no matter how delayed, the offering might have on a person.

Do I need to tell recipients to treat the Rosary with reverence?

When presenting the Rosary, even to a person who is not a Catholic, I have never felt the need to say more than "This is filled with prayers." I think that alone implies that the Rosary is special.

In the beginning, it crossed my mind a number of times that perhaps I should tell the recipient that the physical Rosary was but an outward sign of Mary's grace and had no intrinsic spiritual power. I worried that someone, especially someone not acquainted with our faith, might use it as a kind of talisman. But then I brought the matter up to Mary who reminded me that my job was just to deliver a Mother's gift. The rest was between Mary, her Son and that soul.

Is there a limit to how many Rosaries I can give out?

Some years I have prayed over dozens of strands. Other years, just a few. It's important to remember that it is the sincerity of your prayers for the intentions of a particular recipient that counts; not how many Rosaries you give out.

Taking the First Steps

If you have spent time in prayer and have decided to accept Mary's call to become a minister for the Ministry of the Holy Rosary, I welcome you into this very special brotherhood/sisterhood of prayer.

Through your commitment, souls in need of God's tender mercies will find new faith. As you extend the offer of a Rosary filled with the intercessory prayers said on their behalf, the message rings clear. This was no chance meeting. No random act. God knows of their plight and has sent you to remind them of His great power to save. You can offer no greater gift.

The Importance of the Sacrament of Reconciliation

There aren't many of us who can maintain a state of grace for any length of time. Today's fast-paced world is filled with challenges. Although we may immediately repent of our ill tempers, harsh words and unchristian thoughts, the stain of sin creates a distraction that draws us away from our mission. Our peace is shattered. We meet a neighbor we recently gossiped about and feel a pang of conscience. Even though we have asked God's forgiveness, the feelings of guilt or unrest remain. This can only be exorcised through a sincere and heartfelt confession.

When we approach the Sacrament of Reconciliation, we must begin by searching our consciences. This allows the Holy Spirit to highlight areas in our lives that we might not have been aware should be addressed. Once these are uncovered, confessed and then absolved through the Sacrament of Reconciliation, we find ourselves more in tune with the Holy Spirit, which enables us to be more effective instruments of God's peace.

The Need to Receive the Eucharist

How blessed we are as Catholics to be able to physically meet Jesus through the Eucharist. It is the most powerful of moments, the joining of the mystical with our lowly state, transforming us into the image of God's most Holy Son. At that moment, we are no longer separated by time and space, but are one. How blessed. How divine.

Lately it appears that just about every talk show or magazine is discussing the importance of one's diet. Maintaining a balanced diet is key to a healthy, vibrant, disease-free lifestyle, we're told. "You are what you eat," is the refrain.

Well, that can also be said about the Eucharist.

The more often we meet Jesus through the Eucharist, the more our spiritual lives will remain vibrant and healthy, providing us with the spiritual strength needed to make it through the myriad issues we all must face—failing health, the death of a loved one, the loss of a job, difficult relationships. The list is endless. This daily dose of spiritual nourishment equips us to handle these challenges. It strengthens us to better live out the tenets of our faith, one of which is God's edict to spread the message of His great love through compassion and evangelization.

Receiving the host daily also heightens our ability to 'hear' the Holy Spirit when we're prompted to pray for a certain grace … healing, reconciliation, peace … over a particular Rosary. As I said before, I'm always awed when I discover that that particular grace was exactly what was needed by the recipient who was later sent my way.

Seeking Priestly Counsel

With the growing shortage of priests, I am always hesitant to add to a priest's already overtaxed schedule by asking him to act as my spiritual director; yet, whenever I have needed guidance for this ministry, priestly counsel has always helped me to sort things out. Through their Godly counsel, I find myself better equipped to serve the Blessed Mother and those whom she places across my path.

Their Godly counsel is especially helpful when I feel discouraged or during those times when months go by and no one is sent across my path. Often, I will begin to doubt my calling. Kindly priests have taught me to use these pauses to reevaluate my personal journey and make course adjustments when necessary. Most of all, they have taught me to ask the hard questions ...

Have I allowed myself to think too highly of my role in this ministry, or my place among God's other servants? Is there a hidden sin that is preventing Mary from using me?

I then do the inner work that must be done, ask for forgiveness and pick up the ministry and go on. Just remember that, when you are in doubt of your effectiveness for God through this ministry, do not give up. *"The One who calls you is faithful ..."* (I Thess.5:24) Whatever the issues you must resolve, do not grow discouraged. You are not alone. All the resources of Heaven are at your disposal.

Keeping a Journal

I have a bookshelf filled with prayer journals that I have kept for more than 30 years. Nothing fancy. Some are cloth bound, but most are plain spiral notebooks.

In the beginning, these journals were a way to help clarify my thoughts, focus on areas that I wished to understand or chart my spiritual growth.

I continued my journaling as I began to pray over strands of Rosaries. I place the date when I finish praying and the particular grace if the Holy Spirit has prompted me to pray. Once the recipient arrives, I jot down the story describing our meeting. I then leave a space before starting a new entry, which can later be filled in should any stories filter back on how that Rosary has impacted a life.

I have prayed over countless Rosaries down through the years. Sometimes, I might feel too tired to continue my prayers, or discouraged because a recipient hasn't appeared for several months. That's when I thumb through my journals and find renewed passion for this ministry, as I find stories such as ...

A man given up by doctors suddenly stumbles upon another course of treatment through which he is healed when given a Rosary; or a woman who wrote to say that, in the midst of her troubled world, she now finds great peace through Mary's special gift of the Rosary.

These journals also have come to attest to how this ministry has helped me to better evangelize my faith by spilling over into other areas of prayer.

One recent entry recounts the story of a man who was working at a farm stand. I saw that he was in a great deal of back pain. Without hesitation, I found myself asking him if I might offer a prayer of healing on his behalf. He nodded his consent, so I placed a hand on his shoulder and prayed with an earnest heart, not at all uncomfortable or embarrassed as other customers went about paying for their purchases. (I even noticed a few had bowed their heads and joined in.)

This was something that I would never have done before Mary called me to this ministry. Imagine, a Catholic layperson praying for someone in public!

But through this wonderful ministry, Mary has taught me how to offer a heartfelt prayer to anyone, anywhere in need; a gift that I have surprisingly found is warmly embraced in a world that has grown so indifferent to the pain and suffering of others.

Presenting the Rosary

Once you have finished your intercessory prayers, slip the Rosary into your purse or pocket where it will be easily accessible when Mary calls you to present her gift.

That first time may be a little frightening. I remember how scared I was the day Mary asked me to present my silver Rosary to the homeless woman. A plethora of fears flashed across my mind.

What if she refused them?

What if someone was watching? What would they think?

What if I couldn't think of something to say to convey the meaning behind the Rosary?

What if someone I knew saw me doing this and labeled me a religious zealot?

When plagued by such misgivings, remember: Mary has called you to this ministry. You didn't 'just happen' across this book, or that talk or presentation. You were specially chosen. And because you were chosen, Mary will see that you are well equipped through the gifts of her blessed Spouse, the Holy Spirit.

Just walk through your fears and rely on our Holy Mother. She never fails to lead. ॐ

Author's Note:

Twenty-plus years ago, I gave away a cherished Rosary to a homeless woman in a gesture of the Father's great love. Two people were transformed that day. The woman filled with hopelessness and despair, to the revelation that she was greatly loved by God. And me from a person who felt that she had little to offer the Lord, to a bearer of the most powerful source of intercessory prayers reflected by a strand of beads.

Since that day, I have prayed over and given away hundreds of Rosaries. Each has been prayed over for the intentions of an anonymous person in need of comfort whom Mary would send across my path. The scenario is always the same. A chance meeting. A person who begins to share with me their sorrow or fears or despair. A familiar *push* that signifies this is the person for whom the Rosary is intended. I offer the Rosary. Hands reach out to embrace the gift.

"This is filled with prayers," I say. "I hope it gives you comfort."

The reaction is always the same. Tears. Disbelief at this physical sign of God's great compassion. How else would one explain my just happening along at this particular time and place in order to meet them, bearing a gift of prayers that had been said on their behalf?

Over the years, stories have filtered back. Some truly amazing. Others deeply poignant. All filled with the touch of God's grace and a Mother's compassion.

In 2008, on the first Sunday of Advent, I was awakened by Mary's voice speaking to my heart.

Take my Ministry of the Holy Rosary to the world.

Inner voices can be tricky. After all, how do we know that what we 'hear' is not our own voice? Having been down this road many times through this personal ministry, I knew that if this was truly Mary's will, the people and events needed to bring this to pass would follow without any prompting of mine. So, I waited.

Meanwhile, I contacted a dear priest friend who had been blessing these Rosaries for years and even had a story of his own associated with one of these special strands. I told him what I felt Mary wanted me to do. I also passed along a Novena that I had designed specifically for the ministry which he quickly approved.

Then he said it was strange that I should bring up this ministry. He said that for weeks, every time he prayed the Rosary, he would had an inner picture of me wearing a white turtleneck and blue sweater, seated in an overstuffed chair with eyes closed as I prayed the Rosary. Then he would hear Mary's voice saying, *Tell her to open her eyes.*

It just so happened that it was winter, and most mornings I prayed my Rosary seated in an overstuffed chair, wearing a white turtleneck and a blue sweater. Coincidence? I figured not.

If Mary's edict to 'open my eyes' meant that it was time to look outside of myself and share this ministry, I would need my bishop's approval. Before I went to the bishop, I would need to inform my parish priest what I intended to do. "It will never happen," he replied when I outlined my plan. "The bishop is much too busy with other matters. But go ahead and send it along if you'd like."

My priest was right. It was the middle of the firestorm that centered on the sex scandals that had rocked our Church. The bishop was indeed busy. The chance that he might take time out of his enormously hectic schedule to review my proposal was slim. In fact, the only way that I could imagine that happening was if Mary personally intervened. I sent up a prayer and mailed my request.

A few weeks later, I opened my mailbox to discover a letter bearing the Archbishop seal. I laid it on the kitchen counter and made a cup of strong tea before finding the courage to open it. I read it through twice before the words sank in. The bishop had given his approval for the ministry and assured me of his continued prayers for its success. Once again Mary had proven herself equal to the task.

But, now what? How does one launch a lay ministry? I pondered the question for weeks.

Then one day while walking the dogs, I had an idea. I was a writer. What if I were to create an instructional book that spelled out the program details? Once the book was published, it would support a round of lectures to formally announce the ministry.

I was just about to write up an outline to send on to New York, when Mary spoke to my heart. *You are to discharge your literary agent.*

Let me pause here to explain that this suggestion was absolutely ludicrous. The literary agency that represented me was one of the top in New York City. Any writer would have killed to be listed among its roster filled with illustrious, best-selling clients, and yet, Mary was telling me to leave?

Granted that my agent had been trying to get me to write more-secular material *and* my priest friends kept insisting that I should go back to my original calling, which was to write faith-based books. But give up on this agency just when I would need an agent to market the book I was writing for Mary's ministry? It made absolutely no sense.

By the first of December, I could no longer sidestep the issue and so, in obedience to Mary, I left the literary agency that had represented me for eight years. I was now an author without representation with a book that I needed to publish to get this ministry off the ground. Publishers will only consider manuscripts submitted by established literary agents, so by ditching my agent, it seemed like I was being asked to make bricks with no straw. But once again, I had factored out Mary.

On December 21, I received an e-mail from an acquisitions editor at a major Catholic publishing house. She asked if I would be interested in writing a book geared toward the teenage audience. I wrote back to say that the teenage audience was not my forte, however, there was another book that I had in mind based on the Rosary. I then began to share the story of the homeless woman and how that gift had become the impetus behind a personal ministry that had since deeply touched the lives of hundreds of recipients. Would she be interested in a book that explained the ministry and invited others to join?

The next day I received this e-mail from the editor:

"I presented your concept to the Editorial and Marketing Boards today and they are 100% enthusiastic and would like to move forward."

Apparently when you work with Mary there is no need for an agent.

Now that I had a contract, I was eager to begin; yet unlike a novel where the characters just show up and I follow along, I would have to stick to a well-thought out series of topics that explained the how and why this ministry worked. I would have to base my statements on Biblical truths supported by the stories of the effect these

Rosaries had on the recipients. It was so different from what I was accustomed to write that I developed a major case of writer's block.

No matter what I wrote, it didn't truly represent what I felt in my heart. As an established author, I knew when my writing engaged the reader and this definitely did not. For the next several weeks, I wrote and deleted, wrote and deleted until my confidence in the book plummeted.

One morning, I was seated at our old, scarred kitchen table, my hands cupped around a half-empty mug of cold coffee, feeling confused and angry.

"What made me think that I could write a book about this ministry?" I asked my husband Paul. "I'm a novelist, not a Catholic theologian."

"Apparently, Mary thinks you can," Paul said, refilling my coffee mug and smiling a smart-alecky grin.

"Then, she must have gotten me mixed up with of them," I said, pointing to stacks of Catholic based books that filled every empty space in several rooms. I had figured if I was to write a Catholic non-fiction book, I should see how others did it. The research, however, had only further shaken my confidence.

"Those authors have studied Catholic doctrine and theology. I could never write a book that came up to those standards," I moaned, dropping my face into my hands. "I'll just have to call my editor and ask to withdraw the manuscript." The statement turned my stomach into knots.

I was a seasoned writer and had written for some of New York's largest publishing houses. From experience, I knew that, once a book was scheduled for release, a lot of time and money had already been put into a project. As a professional writer, I was mortified that I was about to dishonor my contract, something I had never done before.

At that moment, the dogs spied a squirrel outside and were about to lunge through a glass door. Paul rushed to let them outside while I took my Bible and coffee, shuffled back to our bedroom, and fell into my overstuffed 'prayer' chair.

The house had grown so quiet that I could hear the basement furnace click on. I grabbed my Bible and tried to settle my thoughts. I felt mentally bruised from the creative war that had raged for weeks. I randomly flipped open my Bible. My eyes fell on Deuteronomy 30:11.

"Now, what I am commanding you today is not too difficult for you or beyond your reach..."

It was definitely one of those 'God-incidences' moment that sent a chill up my spine. What were the odds that I would open to that page?

Suddenly, I no longer felt despondent. In fact, I had a sudden revelation. I had been trying to write like *other* Catholic authors, but Paul was right. Mary had not called them to write her book. She had called me. And my writing style is that of a storyteller, similar to that of her Son Jesus, who often couched spiritual lessons in parables, a fancy word for sharing insights through a storyline.

I rushed back to my office, erased the manuscript files and started again. Suddenly, the book began to take on a voice of its own. I was once again back into the flow, feeling more like a transcriber than the creative source.

You're holding that book right now.

Many good-intentioned people have told me how they felt Mary wanted this ministry presented. I, however, have learned never to second-guess anything related to God. Instead, I stayed true to the mission she placed on my heart.

That meant it was a ministry created to comfort the suffering by delivering a message, through a Rosary filled with prayers said specifically for the recipient's intentions. It was also to be a non-denominational ministry. After all, Mary is the Universal Mother. Her love knows no religious or social boundaries. She is a shining example of 'love all and judge no one.'

Having said that, I watched with dismay as two separate publishers who had purchased the manuscript, backed out once they saw it. They felt it did not meet their doctrinal guidelines. (Both, however, allowed me to keep the advances that later became the seed money to start my own publishing house, DP Publishing —named after my grandson and best buddy, Daniel Patrick— which goes to prove, never underestimate the power of Mary and of the Rosary.)

From the very beginning, the people and talents that were needed just seemed to appear. Like the photographers Catherine and Vinnie Montalbano, who created this wonderful cover. (If you wish to read the story behind the cover, go to my blog at http://blog.katherinevalentine.com/.)

Next on board was a neighbor, friend and dynamite editor, Eileen Denver, who for many years headed the editorial department of Consumer Reports. (She has even appeared on Oprah… twice! Does Mary know how to pick them or what?!) There were also those who 'arrived' when needed to format the manuscript, printers and graphic artists also showed up at just the right time. And I am deeply indebted to our son, Matthew, who just happens to be a genius at marketing and at things Internet-related and worked tirelessly to get the word out to 'the world.'

As always, there is my dear husband, *Saint* Paul who has supplied endless cups of tea along with support. And at moments when my faith has wavered and I felt certain that this venture would never fly, he has reminded me of all the other times when we were faced with impossible situations and how God sent along a miracle of sometimes epic proportions. (I'm putting that story in book form now to encourage others not to give up on their dreams.)

In my purse and on my mirror are index cards that bear a response God once gave me to an urgent prayer request. *Haven't I proved time and time again that I am greater than your needs?*

The fact that you're reading this book is the ongoing evidence to that promise and a message of hope that I share with all my readers.

Peace and Joy,

Katherine Valentine
Woodbury, CT, April, 2012

The Gift is destined to capture the hearts of all those who have sought to be of service to the Lord but have lacked a path until now....

$9.99 US/$10.99 Canada

Available through
www.katherinevalentine.com
e-book available at
Amazon.com

Share Mary's special lay ministry of *The Gift* with others through your church*, book clubs and friends.

You may also order by mail. Please complete the form below:

Name: _____

Address: _____

City: _____ State: _____ ZIP: _____

Quantity: _____

Per copy:
Price: $ 9.99
Shipping US: $ 2.96
(CT Residents please   ($ 0.64)
include sales tax.)   _____

                Total: _____

Make checks payable to: DP Publishing
Mail to Address: P.O. Box 608
                         Woodbury, CT   06798

* For discount information on orders of over 50 please contact:
katherine.valentine@yahoo.com